The 5-Bucket Budget

The 5-Bucket Budget

A practical method to organize your money and build wealth

Daniel Hayes

Mindful Pages

Published in 2025

ISBN: 9789371771894 (PB)
ISBN: 9789371778503 (eBook)

Published by

Mindful Pages
Imprint of Alpha Editions LLC
312 W. 2nd St #1834
Casper, WY 82601, USA

This book was developed using advanced writing tools to support the drafting and ideation process. All content has been thoughtfully curated, refined, and reviewed to ensure quality and relevance.

Content

Introduction
Money Without the Fog

Most people don't falter with money because they are careless; they falter because the tools they are given are misaligned with reality. Conventional budgeting—spreadsheets, apps, rigid percentage rules—promises control but often delivers frustration. It treats finances as arithmetic, when in truth, managing money resembles cartography more than calculation. Our financial lives are uneven, messy, emotional, and constantly shifting. What we need is not another formula, but a map that adapts, orients, and illuminates without overwhelming.

This book offers such a map.

The 5-Bucket Budget is not a doctrine of austerity, nor a gospel of optimisation. It is a reimagining of money management—how we assign meaning to money, organise it with intention, and make decisions in partnership with life's inherent unpredictability. Whether you are a freelancer with irregular income, a couple juggling competing priorities, or a salaried professional perpetually wondering where the month went, this approach meets you without judgement and with clarity.

At its heart, the 5-Bucket method recognises why most traditional budgets fail: they assume income is stable, expenses are predictable, and willpower alone can sustain long-term financial behaviour. Life, it turns out, is rarely that obedient. Budgets fail not because of individual weakness but because the model is brittle. Conventional approaches demand relentless tracking, perfect foresight, and constant self-policing—and when reality deviates, they leave a residue of guilt. The system is at fault, not the user.

The 5-Bucket Budget introduces a framework that is robust yet breathable, clear yet flexible. It delineates five functional categories—Essentials, Growth, Safety, Joy, and Overflow—not as arbitrary labels but as reflections of the actual roles money plays in our lives. This is grounded not in theory alone, but in cognitive science, behavioural economics, and lived experience.

If you have ever felt, "I earn too much to feel this stressed," or, "I don't even know where my money goes," this method is designed for you. If previous attempts at budgeting collapsed within weeks, it was not due to indiscipline but misalignment with human behaviour. Traditional budgeting obsessively tracks every penny, yet such precision rarely produces control; instead, it generates fatigue, resentment, and disengagement.

The 5-Bucket approach begins from a different premise: clarity, not rigidity, is the pathway to financial control. Clear categories reduce the number of micro-decisions, and giving money purpose upfront diminishes mental overhead downstream. Functional allocation replaces forensic tracking; purpose supplants micromanagement.

We first explore why conventional budgets break—not through mathematical error, but structural flaw. Income volatility, unpredictable expenses, moral binaries between spending and saving, and the unseen cognitive costs of constant micro-management all conspire to render plans obsolete. Against this backdrop, the 5-Bucket framework aligns more faithfully with reality.

Its beauty lies in flexibility. Unlike static rules—spend 30% on housing, save 20% for retirement—the 5-Bucket Budget scales across life stages, income levels, and changing goals. It accommodates irregular cash flows, windfalls, and lean periods without collapsing. Its power is not prescriptive; it allows you to observe patterns, then make intentional choices.

Each bucket serves a distinct role: Essentials define true necessity; Growth fuels future wealth through investing, learning, or asset-building; Safety becomes a proactive architecture of resilience; Joy is deliberately prioritised, recognised as vital rather than indulgent; Overflow functions as a diagnostic tool, revealing imbalances without judgement.

Yet this system is not merely structural—it is behavioural. Financial health emerges from designing environments that make good choices easier. We examine how habits form, how friction undermines intention, and how small behavioural cues can drive substantial outcomes. The 5-Bucket model is integrated not as a temporary fix but as a durable framework.

It is not a fire drill. It does not promise immunity from setbacks. Instead, it equips you to respond effectively when life intervenes. Job loss, medical emergencies, major transitions—these are constants, not anomalies. The 5-Bucket Budget prepares you to navigate them with composure and minimal emotional wear.

This approach balances pragmatism with humanity. It honours emotion, acknowledges trade-offs, and treats money as more than numbers—recognising its influence on security, dignity, identity, and possibility. A good financial system does not constrain life; it enlarges it.

Unlike many personal finance ideologies, this one avoids austerity fetishisation and moralising. It does not equate financial independence with virtue or sacrifice with success. It champions intentionality: spending, saving, investing, and protecting resources in alignment with values. Wealth becomes a state of clarity, choice, and confidence, not a mere numeric milestone.

In the chapters ahead, theory is paired with practice. You will find frameworks, case studies, decision tools, and implementation guides. But more than tools, this book provides a way of thinking—a way to see money clearly, organise it coherently, and act with agency rather than obligation.

This is not about creating the perfect budget. It is about cultivating a confident steward of your financial life. The 5-Bucket Budget is your compass—flexible, human-centred, and designed to grow with you. It restores agency, reduces friction, and equips you to navigate both abundance and scarcity with intention.

Let's begin.

Chapter 1
Why Budgets Break

It is a curious irony of modern life that something as measurable as money remains so widely misunderstood. We carry figures in our minds—salaries, mortgage balances, monthly bills—yet the systems we use to govern them often rest on myth rather than lived experience. Chief among these myths is the idea of financial control. Most budgeting advice presents control as mastery: stable inputs, predictable outputs, and the comforting belief that if you follow the plan, results will follow. But ask anyone who has tried to "stick to the plan" and a familiar narrative emerges: a job changes, a boiler breaks, a family obligation interrupts, a pandemic strikes. The spreadsheet, inevitably, did not foresee it.

This, in essence, exposes the foundational flaw in conventional budgeting. They mistake stability for normalcy and treat deviation as failure. The core assumption is linearity: money in, money out, managed by discipline and foresight. Yet personal finance is not an engineering problem—it is behavioural. Life is in constant flux: jobs fluctuate, expenses spike, goals evolve, partners disagree, health changes, and economies wobble. Elegant theoretical models collapse under the weight of reality—not because we lack intelligence or willpower, but because the frameworks themselves were brittle from the start.

Consider the archetypal monthly budget: a meticulously colour-coded document, each category pre-defined, every expense accounted for. Rent, groceries, transport, dining, entertainment—perhaps a token savings allocation if anything remains. It promises order but demands precision. It expects petrol bills to remain constant, reimbursements to arrive on time, invitations to be predictable. It assumes life will behave.

Life, however, does not conform to formulas. The babysitter cancels, necessitating emergency childcare. The laptop fails three weeks before a critical project deadline. A teenager breaks an ankle playing football. A sudden surge of generosity prompts a lavish dinner for a partner. These are not financial crises—they are life. Yet in rigid frameworks, they register as anomalies, as failures to adhere to the plan.

The deeper problem is that traditional budgets cast deviation as dysfunction. Over time, this framing exacts a psychological toll: people feel guilty for being human. They assess their spending not through values or context, but through a binary lens of success versus failure. On budget or off; disciplined or wasteful; responsible or reckless. These narratives do more harm than help.

Enter the binary trap, a pervasive feature of financial discourse. Every pound becomes a moral choice: save and you are virtuous; spend and you are indulgent. Asceticism is sanctified; consumption condemned. Advice such as "cut out coffee" or "live like a student" embodies this logic. The implicit promise: abstinence equates to financial salvation. Yet money is not moral—it is a tool, a medium of exchange, a means to shape experience. Decisions are rarely binary; they are nuanced, often emotional, and situated within trade-offs invisible on a ledger. A parent outsourcing meals may appear "wasteful" in a spreadsheet, yet this decision preserves sanity, sustains family engagement, and protects health.

What is required, then, is a budgeting model attuned to the richness of human motives—one that honours context, complexity, and the subtleties of choice. Saving is not always possible; spending is not always reckless. Decisions are negotiations between needs, emotions, opportunities, and risks. They cannot be reduced to slogans. The system must support, guide, and clarify, rather than shame or constrain.

Even when traditional budgets are technically followed, the cognitive overhead is immense. Tracking, categorising, and updating each transaction generates a relentless mental load. What began as organisation becomes administration. Psychologists term this decision fatigue: the erosion of mental energy from repeated small choices. The more attention demanded by minutiae, the less remains for significant decisions. Budgets fail not in crisis, but in quiet exasperation—they exhaust those who attempt them.

Cognitive science offers further insight. Working memory can hold roughly four to seven items at a time. This is evolution, not flaw; simplicity preserves attention. Traditional budgets fragment focus across dozens of micro-categories, demanding juggling of petrol versus train fare, groceries versus toiletries, subscriptions versus utilities. The outcome is not mastery but clutter.

By contrast, grouping by function rather than form reduces cognitive load. Rather than asking whether spending counts as "dining out" or "entertainment," a function-based model considers its role: does it serve survival, growth, safety, joy, or overflow? This subtle shift mirrors natural prioritisation, aligning with how people actually think.

Thus emerges the five-bucket model. Money is allocated across five functional categories: Essentials for living and obligations; Growth for future investments, education, and asset building; Safety to buffer volatility; Joy to sustain pleasure, dignity, and emotional health; Overflow as a diagnostic lens, signalling imbalance or opportunity. The model reflects life as it is—fluid, nuanced, and human—rather than life as a spreadsheet demands it to be.

This approach does not abandon structure; it redefines it. Structure must fit human psychology, emotion, and behaviour. A system that collapses under pressure is not a system—it is an untested hypothesis. Good financial systems bend, adapt, and recalibrate. They survive not through perfection, but through flexibility.

Flexibility is not weakness; it is the foundation of control. The capacity to adjust, absorb shocks, and reallocate resources constitutes true mastery—durable clarity achieved through functional design, not brittle precision.

As this chapter unfolds, we will deconstruct long-held illusions in personal finance, examine why most budgets fail psychologically as well as technically, and explore how real people make decisions in complex, unpredictable lives. By the end, you will understand why conventional models falter—and why the five-bucket approach endures.

Money, after all, is more than currency. It is the architecture of choice, the vocabulary of priorities, and the medium through which agency is built—or rebuilt. It is time to give that architecture the strength it deserves.

The Myth of Financial Control

The idea that we can fully control our finances is a seductive fiction—comforting, intuitive, and almost universally false. It rests on a premise that feels reasonable: that with sufficient discipline, foresight, and effort, money can be managed into compliance. Yet in practice, this belief collapses under the weight of daily unpredictability. Most budgeting systems assume stability as their default setting—steady income, fixed expenses, predictable behaviours. But life does not offer such terms. It is fluid, erratic, and often uninterested in the constraints we attempt to place upon it. The moment we treat money as a static system, we lose touch with the reality of how it moves through real lives.

To understand why so many budgets fail, we must start with what they assume. Traditional personal finance frameworks operate on a logic borrowed more from engineering than from psychology. They are built around the notion that if you measure and control each component—track every expense, allocate every category—you will produce a reliable result. But people are not machines. Our incomes fluctuate, our priorities evolve, and our behaviours are shaped less by calculation than by context, emotion, and experience. A budget, however sophisticated, cannot deliver stability in a world that doesn't offer it. And yet, when a plan fails, we rarely blame the plan. We blame ourselves.

This is the silent cruelty of the financial control myth: it turns complexity into character failure. When someone overspends after a stressful week, they are labelled undisciplined. When emergency expenses derail savings goals, the story becomes one of poor planning. When income drops unexpectedly, it's often framed as a temporary disruption rather than a structural risk. But what if the problem is not the individual, nor the exception, but the entire assumption? What if the flaw lies in treating personal finance as a game of control, when in fact it should be one of adaptation?

Real control—durable, sustainable control—does not come from precision. It comes from resilience. This distinction is not merely semantic; it is foundational. Precision seeks perfection. It assumes that if we get the inputs right—calculate carefully, plan thoroughly, behave consistently—the outputs will follow suit. But resilience understands that the world is unpredictable. It anticipates disruption. It does not depend on ideal conditions. Instead, it builds systems that bend without breaking.

Consider the lived experience of a young professional on a modest salary. They begin the year with good intentions: a detailed budget, automated savings, perhaps even a debt repayment plan. For the first few months, all goes well. Expenses are tracked, spending stays within boundaries, the numbers add up. Then reality arrives. A flatmate moves out unexpectedly, doubling their rent. A dental emergency wipes out their emergency fund. Their work offers inconsistent hours. Within weeks, the budget is obsolete, the goals feel naive, and guilt begins to accumulate. They are not alone. Research consistently shows that most people abandon strict budgets within the first three to six months. The reason is not laziness—it is misalignment between expectation and experience.

Life, by design, defies budgeting assumptions. It is not monthly. It is not symmetrical. The electricity bill spikes in winter. Car insurance renewals hit annually. Christmas distorts spending patterns. Incomes lag behind inflation. A parent falls ill and requires support. These events are not rare—they are representative. A budget that cannot accommodate such realities is not a useful tool; it is a fragile artefact, destined to collapse under pressure.

The solution is not to budget harder. It is to budget differently. Rather than aiming for exhaustive control, we must build systems that reflect how money actually behaves in real lives. That means replacing rigidity with adaptability, replacing micro-management with functional clarity, and replacing guilt-driven narratives with psychologically sustainable structures.

The illusion of financial control also thrives on another faulty assumption: that money decisions are primarily rational. Behavioural economics has spent decades dismantling this belief, demonstrating that we are not economic calculators, but meaning-making creatures shaped by context, identity, and emotion. We spend to feel safe, to express love, to manage stress, to claim autonomy. These motivations do not show up in budgeting spreadsheets. But they drive the very behaviours budgets are trying to control.

When a parent buys an expensive gift for their child despite a tight budget, it may not be poor planning—it may be an attempt to offset guilt from long working hours. When someone spends impulsively after a breakup, it is not financial recklessness—it is emotional regulation. These actions, viewed in isolation, appear irrational. But in context, they often make deep psychological sense. Any financial system that fails to acknowledge this will always feel adversarial. It will punish what it cannot understand.

This is why flexibility is not a concession—it is a design imperative. Flexibility allows for complexity. It accommodates the fluctuations in our emotional landscape, our career trajectory, our relationships, and our health. It does not mean chaos; it means capacity. The capacity to adjust, to reallocate, to re-prioritise in response to changing conditions. A flexible financial system assumes change, rather than resisting it.

This is not a theoretical abstraction. In practice, a flexible approach means shifting from line-item rigidity to purpose-based categorisation. It means thinking less in terms of *how much did I spend on transport?* and more in terms of *is my spending aligned with what matters to me?* It means accepting that some months will be lean, others flush, and that the goal is not uniformity, but intentionality over time.

The fragility of traditional budgets also reveals itself in the way they deal with uncertainty. Most budgeting tools project the past into the future: if you spent £150 on groceries last month, plan for the same this month. But this approach cannot account for irregularities—nor can it handle the emotional toll of constantly monitoring small variances. When you overspend, even slightly, you feel you've broken the plan. When you underspend, the surplus often disappears unaccounted. Over time, these fluctuations erode trust in the system itself. And when the system fails, people don't rebuild it—they abandon it.

Contrast this with systems built around *functional buckets*—categories based on the purpose money serves rather than the specific form it takes. Essentials. Growth. Safety. Joy. Overflow. These groupings offer conceptual clarity without demanding constant recalibration. They reflect the actual way people allocate attention: not by differentiating between toiletries and groceries, but by asking whether a purchase is necessary, protective, enriching, or discretionary. This method simplifies decision-making without dumbing it down. It supports consistency without rigidity.

Philosophically, this marks a shift from control to stewardship. Control suggests dominance over variables; stewardship suggests care amid uncertainty. A steward recognises that they cannot eliminate risk, but they can build systems that absorb it. They don't assume every pound will follow a script. Instead, they design a structure in which every pound has a role—even if the details shift.

This approach also reframes failure. Under the myth of control, any deviation from plan is a problem to be corrected. Under a stewardship model, deviations are data points. They reveal changing needs, emotional signals, or system mismatches. They become opportunities to improve alignment, not reasons for self-reproach. This perspective reduces shame—a common, corrosive emotion in personal finance—and replaces it with curiosity and agency.

We must also confront the fact that financial volatility is not an aberration for most people—it is the norm. Gig workers, freelancers, entrepreneurs, single parents, carers, those on benefits, and anyone living without generational wealth face unpredictability as a daily feature. Pretending otherwise is both statistically inaccurate and ethically obtuse. Financial tools must centre these realities, not treat them as edge cases. A system that cannot serve those with irregular incomes, high responsibilities, or complex trade-offs is not a universal tool—it is a luxury product disguised as a solution.

To move beyond the myth of control, we need models that honour the lived experience of financial life. That means integrating behavioural insights, acknowledging systemic constraints, and designing for variability. It means creating systems that hold under pressure—not because they are rigid, but because they are responsive. This is the promise of flexible, purpose-driven budgeting: not the illusion of perfection, but the capacity for coherence amid complexity.

In the end, the goal is not to eliminate volatility, but to navigate it with greater clarity, less stress, and more confidence. Control may be a myth—but wise design is not. The challenge is to stop chasing systems that promise mastery and start building systems that foster movement. Not precision, but direction. Not rigidity, but resilience. That is the foundation of true financial control. And it begins with letting go of the myth.

The Binary Trap: Save or Spend

For all the sophistication with which we now approach nutrition, education, and even time management, our collective thinking about money remains remarkably primitive. It is still framed, all too often, as a moral tug-of-war: save like a monk, or spend like a fool. Financial discipline is cast as virtue; indulgence, as weakness. One is celebrated, the other scorned. And within this narrow framework, every transaction becomes a referendum on character. Did you make the "smart" choice or the "wasteful" one? Did you invest your bonus or fritter it away? Did you resist the holiday or betray your future self for a fleeting pleasure?

This binary—save or spend—is not just intellectually lazy. It is emotionally corrosive and behaviourally misleading. It imposes a stark, either/or logic on decisions that are far more complex, contextual, and layered than the dichotomy allows. It ignores the role of emotion, the influence of social environment, the nuances of timing, and the interplay of competing needs. Worse still, it traps individuals in a perpetual cycle of shame and second-guessing. Every splurge feels like a failure. Every act of restraint feels like a test.

The roots of this binary run deep. For centuries, thrift has been idealised across religious, cultural, and philosophical traditions. From Puritan frugality to Protestant work ethics, from Confucian modesty to the Enlightenment emphasis on self-mastery, the idea that good people delay gratification has shaped not just our economic systems but our internal moral compasses. Saving has become more than a financial strategy—it is a symbolic act. It signals foresight, self-control, and worthiness. Spending, by contrast, is associated with hedonism, irresponsibility, and short-termism. These associations are not neutral; they carry moral weight.

Yet the reality of money decisions belies such simplistic categorisation. Saving is not always wise, and spending is not always foolish. A young entrepreneur investing in a stylish wardrobe may be engaging in a strategic form of self-branding, not mindless consumption. A parent choosing to enrol their child in an expensive extracurricular activity may be making a values-based decision, not squandering resources. A mid-career professional booking a restorative solo retreat may be preventing burnout and preserving long-term productivity. These are not failures of discipline.

They are considered uses of money that acknowledge both current needs and future consequences.

Crucially, the save-versus-spend binary also ignores the concept of *purpose*. Money is not merely to be preserved or expended—it is to be *used*. And use implies function. Not all functions serve the same timeline, nor the same emotional or strategic outcomes. Some uses of money secure the basics of life: shelter, food, healthcare. Others protect against volatility: insurance, emergency funds. Others still enable growth: education, business investments, skills training. Then there are uses that support relationships, mental health, identity, and joy. The value of these uses cannot be fully captured by a binary calculus.

The behavioural sciences offer further clarity on this point. Humans are not rational agents optimising utility. We are emotional creatures managing trade-offs. What we buy, save, or sacrifice is deeply influenced by framing, scarcity, and our momentary emotional state. Studies on decision-making under stress, for example, show that people in high-pressure environments tend to prefer immediate rewards—not because they are irrational, but because their cognitive resources are depleted. For someone navigating financial instability, spending on a small luxury may be less about pleasure and more about asserting dignity in a world that constantly denies it.

This is why blanket advice like "cut discretionary spending" or "prioritise saving at all costs" often fails in practice. It disregards the real constraints and psychological dynamics at play.. Telling a single mother working two jobs to "automate her savings" may sound responsible, but if every pound is already earmarked for essentials or emotional recovery, the advice becomes irrelevant. Conversely, telling a high earner with no dependents to curb their occasional luxury purchases may miss the point entirely—those expenses may be part of a sustainable, intentional financial life.

The binary frame also distorts our understanding of risk. Saving is often positioned as inherently prudent, but hoarding cash in low-interest accounts during periods of high inflation can be a form of silent self-harm. Conversely, spending on preventative healthcare, ergonomic equipment, or time-saving services may look like indulgence but actually reduce long-term financial and physical vulnerability. The same act—spending—can either be a threat or a safeguard, depending on context. Judging it through a moral lens obscures more than it reveals.

Even the language we use to describe money reinforces the binary. "Burning through savings." "Throwing money away." "Living for today." These phrases drip with judgement and imply recklessness, as though any outflow is inherently dangerous. Yet money is *meant* to flow. That is its function. Its power lies in its movement, in its ability to convert intention into reality, opportunity into action. Hoarding without purpose is no more admirable than spending without reflection. The goal is not to dam the river, but to guide its course.

This false dichotomy also limits financial literacy. By presenting money management as a test of restraint, rather than a framework for alignment, it narrows the conversation to avoidance rather than optimisation. Young people are taught to fear credit, delay gratification, and mistrust their instincts—lessons that often lead to avoidance behaviours and missed opportunities. Instead of learning how to evaluate trade-offs, model opportunity cost, or design sustainable systems, they learn to feel guilt. And guilt, unlike knowledge, does not produce effective decisions.

A more functional model must replace the binary with a spectrum—one that evaluates money choices through the lenses of purpose, timing, trade-offs, and sustainability. It must acknowledge that sometimes the best "investment" is in a relationship, a new experience, or an hour of regained time. It must allow for the fact that life's most important decisions are rarely the most efficient. And it must empower individuals to craft money systems that reflect who they are, what they value, and what season of life they inhabit.

Consider a real-world example: a couple in their early forties with two children, both working full-time jobs. They are stable but stretched—mortgage, school fees, ageing parents, and demanding work schedules. They choose to spend a significant portion of their disposable income on a cleaner, a weekly takeaway, and a few weekend getaways a year. On paper, they are not "saving aggressively." But in practice, these decisions reduce friction in their relationship, improve their health, and preserve energy for their careers and family life. Should they be saving more? Possibly. But are they acting irresponsibly? Hardly. Their choices reflect a deliberate trade-off: less financial surplus in exchange for more life bandwidth. That is not financial failure. That is strategic use of resources.

Or take a single 29-year-old freelancer navigating a feast-or-famine income cycle. She invests in a premium co-working membership and a personal coach. To an outsider, these may seem like luxuries. To her, they are business-critical. The co-working space reduces her isolation and builds networking opportunities. The coach improves her rate of client acquisition. Saving every possible pound might delay burnout, but spending selectively allows her to grow her income, enhance stability, and ultimately save more in the long run. Her decisions are not dictated by impulse or recklessness. They are contextual, intentional, and forward-facing.

Such examples are not exceptions. They are the norm when financial behaviour is viewed honestly, without the distorting lens of morality. People are not navigating their finances with spreadsheet logic. They are making choices in complex ecosystems of emotion, risk, relationships, and timing. And any system or philosophy that ignores this complexity will remain, at best, aspirational. At worst, damaging.

What is needed is not another set of commandments, but a new framework—one that expands the menu of financial virtues beyond just restraint. Clarity. Alignment. Adaptability. Sustainability. Agency. These are equally valuable, yet rarely discussed. When the conversation moves beyond save versus spend, these values come into focus. Money decisions are no longer cast as battles between angels and devils, but as strategic, human, and responsive acts.

The 5-Bucket model proposed in this book helps break this binary by assigning roles to money, not rules. It understands that spending on joy is not a breach of discipline but a pillar of wellbeing. That saving for growth is different from hoarding out of fear. That protecting against uncertainty is a proactive act, not a passive one. It offers not just categories, but lenses—ways to see financial decisions in context, not isolation.

And once you stop asking, *"Should I save this or spend it?"* and start asking, *"What is this money for, and how does it serve me now or later?"*—you move from obedience to authorship. You stop performing fiscal virtue and begin practising financial wisdom. And that is the real work of wealth.

The Hidden Cost of Mental Overhead

There's an unspoken burden embedded in most budgeting systems—one that rarely appears on any financial dashboard but silently drains the very motivation required to keep the system alive. It is the cost of mental overhead: the cumulative cognitive effort demanded by tracking every transaction, evaluating every decision, and maintaining constant awareness of one's financial behaviour. This is not a minor inconvenience. It is a central reason why even the most well-intentioned budgeting strategies unravel. People don't abandon their budgets because they are irresponsible or inattentive. They abandon them because the act of constant vigilance is unsustainable.

Cognitive psychology has long recognised the limits of human attention and processing capacity. We are not built to manage infinite variables or to operate as real-time auditors of our daily lives. The theory of decision fatigue, now well-documented in behavioural science, describes how the quality of our choices deteriorates after extended periods of decision-making. The same phenomenon applies to budgeting. Every pound spent, every receipt entered, every category reviewed adds another decision point to an already saturated mental environment. Over time, this leads to emotional depletion, reduced self-regulation, and ultimately, disengagement.

Ironically, the more comprehensive a budget is, the more likely it is to fail. Systems that rely on granular categorisation—£38.50 for groceries, £12.00 for rideshare, £7.75 for coffee—require not only the logging of each transaction but the mental work of deciding where it belongs. Was that sandwich a grocery item or a dining out expense? Does the gym membership fall under health or lifestyle? What about the Amazon purchase that includes both nappies and batteries? These are not trivial questions when asked dozens of times per month. They introduce friction. And friction, in this context, is lethal.

Even apps designed to automate these processes often fall short. While they offer convenience, they do not eliminate the need for constant monitoring and correction. Auto-categorisation is frequently inaccurate. Recurring subscriptions are mislabelled. Transactions are duplicated or missed entirely. The user is still the system's supervisor, just now operating with the added complexity of trusting and then verifying automation. What was promised as simplification becomes another layer of cognitive demand.

This leads to a larger insight: *complexity is not synonymous with control*. In fact, beyond a certain threshold, complexity undermines control by overwhelming our capacity to engage. The more intricate a budgeting system becomes, the less likely it is to be maintained. Human attention is a finite resource. We spend it not only on financial management but on work, family, health, and the thousand micro-decisions that compose daily life. A budget that demands continuous scrutiny competes with every other priority. Eventually, something has to give.

Real-world evidence bears this out. In a 2022 study by the Financial Behaviour Institute, over 68% of respondents who abandoned personal budgeting apps cited "too much maintenance" as the primary reason. Not lack of value. Not scepticism. Just maintenance. The burden of *keeping up* became too great. And once the system was abandoned, it wasn't replaced—it was left behind. Not because participants didn't care, but because the system asked too much.

The assumption that tracking equals discipline is both pervasive and misleading. It suggests that the act of monitoring is inherently virtuous, and that success is simply a matter of willpower. But this ignores the very architecture of human cognition. Monitoring is not neutral—it consumes attention, generates decision fatigue, and diminishes cognitive bandwidth for higher-order thinking. Moreover, it subtly shifts the user's relationship with money. From a tool of empowerment, money becomes a source of anxiety, its every movement scrutinised and evaluated.

This tension is exacerbated by cultural narratives that equate financial vigilance with moral character. The "good budgeter" is portrayed as meticulous, attentive, and self-sacrificing. But in reality, this archetype often cracks under pressure. It is not laziness that causes people to let their systems lapse. It is exhaustion. Mental overhead is not immediately visible, but it accumulates like debt—quietly, steadily, until it triggers collapse.

The problem is not merely psychological. It is structural. Most traditional budgets are built on accounting logic—categorise, reconcile, balance. But humans do not think like accountants. Our brains are wired for pattern recognition, not transaction review. We make decisions based on emotion, social cues, habit, and timing. To impose a forensic auditing model on everyday life is to create a fundamental mismatch between the system and the user. It turns personal finance into a second job—one with no salary, constant oversight, and a high risk of burnout.

This is where functional models offer a powerful alternative. By organising money into broad-purpose categories—essentials, growth, safety, joy, overflow—the system aligns with how people actually think and behave. Rather than evaluating each purchase individually, users assess their financial life at the level of function. Did this month's spending in "joy" feel balanced or excessive? Is the "growth" bucket underfunded relative to personal goals? These are fewer, higher-quality decisions. They reduce mental drag without reducing financial awareness.

It is worth drawing a parallel with nutrition. Just as obsessively counting calories can lead to disordered eating, obsessively tracking every expense can distort one's relationship with money. What begins as an effort to gain control can quickly become a source of stress, guilt, and avoidance. Sustainable nutrition, like sustainable finance, relies on clear principles and flexible structures. It encourages self-awareness without demanding constant measurement. The same ethos applies here: *the goal is clarity, not surveillance.*

Cognitive ergonomics—the study of designing systems that fit the way people naturally think—offers further insight. Effective systems reduce cognitive load by minimising unnecessary choices, providing clear cues, and using consistent structures. The five-bucket model embodies these principles. It removes the burden of categorising every expense, replaces it with purpose-based reflection, and limits the number of categories to match the brain's natural memory capacity. This isn't a compromise. It's a design optimisation.

Importantly, reducing mental overhead does not mean relinquishing responsibility. It means *designing for sustainability*. A budgeting system that requires two hours a week to maintain may work in theory, but it is unlikely to survive the pressures of work, caregiving, travel, or illness. A system that requires fifteen minutes a week—because it uses high-level categories, automates where appropriate, and leverages habit cues—has a far better chance of enduring. In the long term, consistency beats intensity.

There is also a hidden emotional dividend in reducing mental overhead: the restoration of trust. When a budgeting system becomes too complex, people begin to feel like they are constantly behind. They delay reconciling their accounts, avoid opening apps, and start fearing what they might find. This avoidance breeds anxiety and corrodes self-efficacy. But when the system is simple enough to keep up with, that trust is rebuilt. People check in regularly. They adjust in real time. They make decisions from a place of clarity, not confusion.

This is not a minor shift. It is the difference between budgeting as punishment and budgeting as empowerment. Between a model that demands control and one that enables coherence. Mental overhead is rarely discussed in financial discourse, but it is one of the most critical design factors in any money system. Ignore it, and you build fragility. Account for it, and you build resilience.

What ultimately matters is not how detailed your system is, but how often and easily you use it. If your financial tools become sources of fatigue rather than clarity, it's not your willpower that needs upgrading—it's the system that needs redesigning. Budgeting should not be a daily grind of transaction logging. It should be a low-friction, high-trust process that supports reflection, facilitates adjustment, and leaves you with more energy than it consumes.

The cost of mental overhead is real, but avoidable. When budgeting models honour human limitations instead of testing them, they last. And when they last, they work. That is how financial clarity is built—not through exhaustive effort, but through elegant design.

A System That Mirrors Reality

The overwhelming flaw in most budgeting systems is that they treat money as a static equation, not a dynamic behaviour. They are designed as if life proceeds in straight lines, with fixed expenses, consistent income, and neatly categorised spending. But life does not work this way. Income fluctuates, needs shift, emotions intervene, and circumstances override intentions. Any financial framework that cannot accommodate this variability is not just impractical—it is fundamentally disconnected from the human experience.

What's often passed off as "discipline" in traditional budgeting models is, in truth, a form of abstraction. We're taught to break spending into narrowly defined categories: groceries, transport, rent, subscriptions, dining out, pet care. The implicit assumption is that the more granular the categories, the more control we exert. But the opposite is often true. Granularity creates noise. It demands constant vigilance, forces micro-decisions, and builds a picture of financial life that may be accurate in data, but incoherent in meaning. You may know what you spent, but not *why*. You may track the outflows, but lose sight of what they represent.

This is where categorising money by function, not form, becomes transformative. A functional model doesn't ask what something *was*, but what role it *played*. Was the purchase about survival, security, aspiration, joy, or excess? Instead of focusing on what line item a transaction fits into, a functional system focuses on what purpose it served in the broader architecture of your life. That shift—from classification to clarity—recalibrates the entire practice of budgeting. It moves the system closer to how people actually think, behave, and prioritise.

The five-bucket model—Essentials, Growth, Safety, Joy, and Overflow—offers a structure that mirrors real-world complexity without overwhelming the user. These buckets are not arbitrary labels; they are foundational roles that money plays in every life, regardless of income level or background. They map to the psychological and practical dimensions of human experience. *Essentials* represent what you need to function. *Growth* is the mechanism by which you invest in your future. *Safety* ensures resilience against shocks. *Joy* honours quality of life. *Overflow* is a barometer for balance, not a reward for austerity.

By using these five functions as organising principles, the model solves several problems at once. First, it dramatically reduces friction. Instead of debating whether a meal out was dining or entertainment, you recognise it as Joy—or, perhaps, as Essentials if it replaced a necessary meal. This minimises decision fatigue and removes the moral valence that traditional budgets often impose. Second, it provides a narrative lens: you begin to see not just where your money goes, but what it *does*. Your finances become a story of priorities, not just transactions.

Consider a person who pays for a course to upskill in their field. Traditional budgets might struggle with classification: is this education, business, professional development? A functional model has no such confusion. It's clearly Growth. Or take the same person splurging on a weekend getaway after a difficult quarter. That's Joy—an intentional allocation to mental restoration, not an "unnecessary expense." By mapping money to meaning rather than minutiae, the system creates coherence.

This coherence is not just conceptual—it's behavioural. Functional categorisation supports habit formation in ways that traditional budgets can't. According to behavioural psychology, habits form most reliably when they are anchored to identity and context. That is, people are more likely to sustain actions that feel aligned with who they are and what they value, rather than those imposed from the outside. Functional buckets create exactly this alignment. You are no longer acting on a prescribed plan. You are acting on a personal blueprint.

Moreover, the simplicity of five categories aligns with what cognitive scientists call *working memory limits*. The average person can hold only about four to seven discrete items in mind at once. Budgets with dozens of subcategories exceed that limit, leading to avoidance, inconsistency, and eventual collapse. A five-bucket model, by contrast, is cognitively ergonomic. It leverages the brain's natural strengths rather than working against them.

There is also a deeper psychological benefit. Functional budgeting de-emphasises the myth of perfection. Because the focus is on alignment and adaptability rather than exactness, users are less likely to feel that a single deviation constitutes failure. If you overspend in Joy one month, the model encourages recalibration—not guilt. You rebalance, not restart. This resilience makes the system sustainable. It becomes something you can live *with*, not something you try to live *up to*.

Crucially, the five-bucket model is not income-dependent. It works whether you earn £1,500 or £15,000 per month. That's because its purpose is not to dictate specific behaviours, but to organise awareness. Someone on a low income might allocate only 2% to Joy and 1% to Growth, while someone wealthier might dedicate 20% or more to each. But both are using the same lens—one that honours trade-offs, supports clarity, and facilitates intentionality. The framework is scalable, because its logic is universal.

Contrast this with percentage-based rulebooks that dominate much of personal finance literature—"50/30/20", "save 15% for retirement", "spend no more than 30% on housing." These rules assume average conditions, average incomes, average lifestyles. But most people's lives are not average. A young freelancer with irregular income, a single parent in London, or a late-career earner with ageing parents—none of them fit neatly into generic ratios. The five-bucket system doesn't ask them to. It adapts.

It also improves communication. For couples or households managing money together, traditional budgets often become battlegrounds of justification. "Why did you spend £60 on that?" becomes a trigger for defensiveness. But when the conversation is structured around function—"How are we doing in the Joy bucket this month?"—the tone shifts. You are talking about roles, not rules. Trade-offs, not trespasses. This reframing fosters shared ownership rather than surveillance.

The model also excels in accommodating irregularity—something that derails most traditional budgets. When income is variable, or expenses spike unpredictably, standard models break down. Functional buckets, however, provide a steady structure even when cash flow is erratic. You may fund each bucket differently each month, but the buckets remain. They act as placeholders for intent, keeping your system coherent even when the numbers fluctuate. This continuity makes it easier to re-engage after disruptions and to adjust without having to reinvent the entire framework.

Another underappreciated benefit is the diagnostic power of Overflow. Traditional budgets treat surplus as either luck or buffer. In the five-bucket model, Overflow is a signal. A full Overflow bucket might suggest an opportunity to increase Joy or invest in Growth. A low or empty one may indicate overextension in Essentials or Joy. It functions as a feedback loop, helping you detect imbalances before they become problems. This is not about tracking for tracking's sake—it's about insight. A healthy Overflow signals that your system is absorbing life's variability without becoming distorted.

Perhaps most importantly, categorising by function respects complexity without creating confusion. It acknowledges that money is not just transactional—it is emotional, symbolic, strategic. Spending decisions reflect our hopes, fears, obligations, and aspirations. No two purchases are ever truly the same, even if they fall into the same traditional category. The five-bucket model captures this nuance. It doesn't eliminate ambiguity, but it contains it. It gives you a way to engage with the complexity of money without being overwhelmed by it.

What emerges is not just a budget, but a mental model. A way of thinking about money that promotes clarity, reduces stress, and supports meaningful behaviour. This is not a workaround. It is a reframe. A move away from financial systems built for theoretical optimisation and towards ones built for human sustainability. Because ultimately, the best budgeting system is not the most precise one. It's the one that *lasts*. And for a system to last, it must reflect not just your financial life, but your real life. This model does. It is not perfect—but it is *possible*. And more importantly, it is livable.

Chapter 2
The Five Buckets—A New Mental Model

If most budgeting systems stumble when confronted with real life, it is because they confuse classification with clarity. They fragment spending into ever-narrower categories, believing that precision guarantees control. Yet in doing so, they obscure the broader picture. They compel you to track whether a purchase falls under "household" or "personal care," while offering no insight into what that spending actually achieved, disrupted, or supported. Traditional budgets organise money around form rather than function—and that distinction is not merely semantic; it is strategic.

The pivot from form to function is the first principle this chapter explores. Rather than ask what a transaction was—a latte, a streaming subscription, a petrol top-up—the Five-Bucket model asks what purpose it served. Was it essential to keeping life operational? Did it build future value? Did it safeguard against risk? Was it an intentional act of joy? Or was it excess that signalled imbalance in the system? These are functional questions, not bureaucratic ones, and they provide far more actionable insight into how people actually experience money.

At its heart, money derives meaning from its use. Ten pounds spent on lunch might be fuel for the day—or compensation for a draining week. One hundred pounds directed to a course may represent professional growth—or avoidance disguised as productivity. By filtering spending through function rather than label, you begin to see money as an extension of values, priorities, and vulnerabilities, rather than a series of receipts. The Five-Bucket framework operationalises this lens.

The model consists of five categories: Essentials, Growth, Safety, Joy, and Overflow. Essentials cover necessities and obligations—rent, groceries, non-negotiables. Growth fuels the future: investments, education, skills development. Safety builds defences: emergency funds, insurance, buffers against life's volatility. Joy captures discretionary spending that sustains dignity and emotional wellbeing—a category often neglected yet deeply desired. Overflow is diagnostic: it is not "extra" money, but a signal indicating imbalance or untapped opportunity.

This structure is intentional, grounded in psychological insight as well as practical application. Cognitive science reminds us that human working memory is limited: George Miller suggested roughly seven items; later research narrows this to four or five for complex tasks. This is not a flaw but a design feature of the mind. So why construct a budgeting system demanding fifteen or twenty categories when five functional ones suffice?

Five is deliberate: it provides enough granularity to distinguish priorities without overloading the brain. It balances abstraction with specificity, structure with simplicity. With these five, you can perform high-level reviews without spreadsheets or apps, recalibrating with minimal mental friction. Conceptually elegant and operationally sustainable, it respects both the mind and the lived experience of money.

Equally important is adaptability. Unlike rigid, percentage-based systems, the Five-Bucket model does not impose fixed ratios. A young professional may emphasise Growth; a new parent may see Essentials dominate; someone recovering from burnout may temporarily prioritise Joy. The model flexes across life stages, income levels, and shifting goals—maintaining coherence without enforcing rigidity.

Rigid systems collapse under variability: sudden income loss, medical bills, unexpected taxes. They serve perfection, not people. The Five-Bucket framework recognises this, providing scaffolding that supports intention while absorbing life's shocks. Joy can be dialled back in a crisis without guilt; Overflow can be redirected to Safety when uncertainty looms. Seasonal adjustments are possible without undermining trust in the system itself.

The model is practical, not merely theoretical. One useful exercise is sketching a current money map through the five buckets—not by logging every transaction, but by estimating percentages of income allocated to Essentials, Growth, Safety, Joy, and Overflow. Even approximate figures reveal implicit priorities, often unaligned with stated values. Someone prioritising security yet neglecting an emergency fund may realise their money story is written by default, not design. Couples disputing "wasteful" spending may uncover deeper imbalances in Joy allocation. These insights emerge not from meticulous tracking but from a functional perspective.

The buckets interact. Growth investments may reduce future dependence on Safety. Spending on Joy can support mental health, enhancing performance in Essentials.

Overflow signals where resources are underutilised or might be redeployed strategically. This interconnectedness makes the model robust, intelligent, and attuned to life's fluidity.

The Five-Bucket system is more than a framework; it is a worldview. It encourages richer questions: not "Did I stay under my grocery limit?" but "Is my Essentials bucket sustainable?" Not "Can I afford this holiday?" but "What role does this play in my Joy allocation?" These questions are human, nuanced, and aligned with the way people actually think when freed from the accountant's lens.

This chapter lays the groundwork for the rest of the book. We move from critique to construction—from diagnosing what fails to creating something that works. Later chapters examine each bucket in detail, their flexibility in context, and their role in supporting long-term financial and psychological resilience. The insight begins here: rejecting the tyranny of narrow categorisation in favour of a system that mirrors how life is actually lived.

Function over form is not simply a design principle. It is a declaration: your financial system should work with you, not against you; structure should liberate, not constrain; clarity is not about knowing every number, but understanding where your money belongs. Adopt a system aligned with reality, and you move with the current, guided and intentional, free to act with confidence rather than hesitation. This is the promise of the Five-Bucket model—and it is where we begin.

The Core Idea: Function Over Form

If traditional budgeting has failed to deliver financial confidence for most people, it is not because the underlying mathematics are flawed. It is because the entire exercise has been built on a mistaken premise: that money management is primarily about categorisation. Line items, receipts, subcategories, percentage rules—these tools reflect an accounting mindset, one that seeks to control behaviour through structure. But while such precision may be appropriate for corporate finance or forensic auditing, it proves inadequate—often counterproductive—when applied to the fluid, emotionally charged, and often unpredictable terrain of personal life. Most people do not think about their money in rows and columns; they think in needs, risks, ambitions, and desires. What matters, then, is not *how* the money was spent, but *why*.

This is the core shift that the Five-Bucket model introduces: from form to function. Instead of sorting transactions by merchant category codes or traditional expense types, we categorise by the role each pound plays in your life. That distinction—though subtle at first glance—has profound consequences. It moves budgeting away from micromanagement and toward meaning. Instead of asking whether an expense qualifies as "transportation" or "leisure," you consider whether it was essential, whether it supported growth, whether it contributed to safety, whether it provided genuine joy, or whether it should fall into overflow—a signal of surplus or misalignment. The same action—taking a taxi, eating out, purchasing a book—can mean very different things depending on context. Function reveals that context. Form flattens it.

This model is grounded in a view of money not as an abstract medium, but as an active agent in shaping our choices, behaviours, and identities. Essentials, Growth, Safety, Joy, and Overflow are not merely budget labels; they are expressions of five universal roles money plays across income levels, geographies, and life stages. They form the spine of a financial system that reflects how people actually live—not how software expects them to behave.

Essentials refer to your operational base—the non-negotiables that keep your life functioning. Housing, groceries, utilities, transport, childcare, necessary medical care. But even here, function matters. The fact that an expense recurs monthly does not automatically make it essential. A second car, for instance, may be presented as a fixed cost, but under functional scrutiny, it might be reclassified—or reconsidered. The bucket forces a deeper interrogation: is this truly foundational, or simply habitual?

Growth is the most often underfunded category, especially for those who view financial planning solely through the lens of immediate obligations. Yet growth is where wealth is built. It includes investments, education, skill-building, business development, and asset acquisition. Anything that enables your money—or your capabilities—to produce future value lives here. It is not exclusive to high-income earners. A £30 online course that improves your earning potential belongs to Growth just as much as a property acquisition. The question is not the amount, but the function.

Safety captures all money devoted to insulation from volatility—your buffers, reserves, insurances, redundancies, and contingencies. This is the bucket that transforms a setback from a crisis into a speed bump. A properly funded Safety category doesn't guarantee that life won't go wrong, but it does ensure that when it does, you have somewhere to land. This is more than emergency funds—it includes protection strategies tailored to your actual risk profile, which evolves with time.

Joy may be the most radical inclusion in the Five-Bucket framework, precisely because it's the most often neglected in traditional systems. Many budgets treat joy spending as a leak—an indulgence to be minimised. The Five-Bucket model reframes it as maintenance. A life devoid of pleasure, self-expression, or meaningful celebration is not financially virtuous—it's unsustainable. Joy can be small—a weekly coffee with friends—or large—a well-planned holiday. What matters is intentionality. This bucket prevents burnout, resentment, and the kind of deferred living that turns money into a prison rather than a tool.

Overflow is not merely "what's left." It's diagnostic. When your Overflow is growing, it's not just a sign of surplus—it's a prompt to reflect. Is your Safety bucket fully funded? Could Growth be accelerated? Is Joy being neglected? When Overflow is consistently empty or negative, that too is revealing. Perhaps Essentials have expanded beyond necessity. Perhaps Safety is being overlooked. Overflow is your system's way of revealing itself to you. It's not a goal—it's a feedback loop.

This model does not attempt to engineer moral perfection. It doesn't prescribe a rigid split between the five buckets because it recognises that life does not unfold in predictable ratios. What matters is not the exact percentage that goes into each category, but the clarity with which you understand the role your money is playing. One person may put 60% into Essentials, another 30%. For some, Joy may be 5%, for others 20%. The system remains coherent across these differences because its logic is grounded in purpose, not prescription.

By categorising money functionally, we also resolve a key psychological barrier to effective budgeting: ambiguity. One of the reasons traditional budgets cause fatigue is that their categories are often redundant or overlapping. A restaurant expense might belong to "food," "entertainment," or "social." A new pair of shoes could fall under "clothing," "work-related," or "personal." The ambiguity leads to friction—mental effort spent deciding where something belongs. That friction accumulates. Eventually, the system becomes unworkable, not because the numbers don't add up, but because the decisions never end.

Function cuts through this ambiguity. Instead of asking, *What is this?* you ask, *What was this for?* The question is sharper. The answer is easier. The habit is more sustainable.

This orientation also enhances strategic thinking. When you look at your financial life through a functional lens, you begin to make higher-quality decisions—not just about how much to spend, but about what your system is optimised for. You might notice that your Growth bucket is underfed despite ambitious career goals. Or that Joy has disappeared entirely, replaced by low-grade resentment. You might find that Essentials are bloated with legacy costs that no longer reflect your actual needs. These are not accounting insights—they are behavioural ones. And they matter far more than knowing whether you went £10 over budget in "entertainment."

The five buckets also help eliminate moral overtones that too often accompany financial advice. In traditional systems, spending is either "good" (savings, essentials) or "bad" (discretionary, indulgent). But this dichotomy is both intellectually lazy and emotionally punishing. It creates guilt where there should be agency. The Five-Bucket model replaces judgement with structure. Joy spending is not "frivolous"; it's Joy. Growth is not "luxury"; it's an investment. Essentials are not automatically virtuous; they're contextual. Function restores neutrality. And neutrality is the precondition for clarity.

For those managing money in shared contexts—couples, families, business partners—the functional model provides a common language. Instead of arguing about individual purchases, you discuss whether the Joy bucket is aligned. Whether Growth needs rebalancing. Whether Essentials have crept up unnoticed. This shifts the conversation from policing to planning, from accusation to alignment. It replaces tension with structure, and structure with trust.

Importantly, the Five-Bucket model does not eliminate the need for numbers. It reframes their purpose. You still track spending, but you do so at a higher altitude. You're no longer drowning in data—you're scanning for signals. When a bucket deviates significantly from your intention, that prompts reflection and recalibration. This creates a living system: responsive, adaptable, but still directional.

Function over form is not just a budgeting technique—it's a philosophy of design. It asks: *What kind of life are you trying to build, and how can money serve that life in clear, sustainable ways?* It accepts that no two lives are the same, but that every life has patterns—and that those patterns can be mapped, resourced, and supported with elegance rather than exhaustion.

This is not minimalism. It's not austerity. It's clarity. And clarity, in the context of personal finance, is a rare and valuable asset. The Five-Bucket model does not promise perfect control. It offers something more useful: functional coherence, behavioural sustainability, and a money system that finally makes sense because it mirrors what life is actually like. Not a spreadsheet fantasy, but a human reality. Not just tracking, but transformation. Not form, but function.

Why Five Is the Magic Number

One of the most underappreciated principles in systems design—whether in engineering, education, or personal finance—is cognitive friction. The harder a system is to understand, remember, or use consistently, the more likely it is to be abandoned. This principle holds especially true in financial planning, where psychological and behavioural sustainability matter just as much as numerical accuracy. It is not the sophistication of a budget that determines its success—it is whether the human using it can remember it, engage with it, and adapt it under pressure. And that's precisely why five categories—not three, not seven, not ten—is the optimal number for organising personal finances in a way that balances nuance with cognitive ease.

The Five-Bucket model isn't a clever branding decision. It is a product of deliberate constraint, grounded in decades of research into human memory, attention, and behavioural science. In 1956, psychologist George A. Miller published a seminal paper titled *The Magical Number Seven, Plus or Minus Two: Some Limits on Our Capacity for Processing Information*. In it, he argued that the average human can hold roughly seven items in working memory at any one time—give or take two. This discovery was not trivial. It became a foundational principle in psychology, shaping how we think about information architecture, interface design, learning theory, and more.

But the intervening decades have added refinement to Miller's law. More recent cognitive science, particularly in the field of working memory, has suggested that *five* is often the practical upper limit for *simultaneously actionable* categories—especially under conditions of stress, distraction, or emotional fatigue. It's not just how many items the brain can *store*, but how many it can *manage* while still making effective decisions. When you're busy, overwhelmed, or navigating financial uncertainty, your working memory contracts. In those moments, simplicity becomes survival.

Apply this insight to traditional budgeting, and the implications are obvious. Most budgeting templates are bloated. They come with a dozen or more categories—housing, utilities, groceries, dining out, subscriptions, transportation, health, insurance, savings, entertainment, debt repayment, clothing, personal care, education, and so on. For each, users are expected to track, review, adjust, and often reconcile. This creates not just complexity but *cognitive drag*—a constant pull on mental bandwidth. The result? Budgeting becomes another administrative burden. Even with good intentions, most people disengage. The system collapses not because of ignorance or irresponsibility, but because it demands more attention than most lives can spare.

The Five-Bucket model eliminates this drag by consolidating transactions into *functions*, not forms. Instead of treating every expense as its own category, we ask: What role did this money play? Did it support your survival (*Essentials*)? Invest in your future (*Growth*)? Insulate you from risk (*Safety*)? Sustain your wellbeing (*Joy*)? Or remain unassigned (*Overflow*)? These five categories are sufficient to capture every financial decision meaningfully, without overwhelming the user. The buckets are distinct enough to cover the full spectrum of money's utility, yet limited enough to remain cognitively portable—you can keep the entire system in your head.

Critically, this design also leverages a second psychological principle: *chunking*. Chunking refers to the brain's ability to group individual items into larger units for easier processing. For example, we don't remember the number 2-0-2-4 as four digits—we remember it as "twenty twenty-four," a meaningful chunk. The same process applies to money. A hundred line items across dozens of spending categories are not manageable. But grouping those into five overarching functions transforms data into insight. Instead of hundreds of financial decisions to track, you have five patterns to observe. That shift makes reflection feasible, habit formation possible, and system longevity realistic.

Another advantage of five is that it allows for strategic tension between categories—enough contrast to provoke useful questions, without overwhelming you with options. For example, you can examine the relationship between *Joy* and *Growth*: are you consistently favouring short-term pleasure at the expense of long-term benefit? Or are you delaying all gratification in a way that's eroding motivation and quality of life? Similarly, *Essentials* versus *Safety* invites a reckoning with over-commitment: are you spending too much on fixed obligations to build a proper buffer against uncertainty? With ten or twelve categories, these patterns are harder to discern. With five, they become visible—and actionable.

This framework is also highly resilient under pressure. When life gets chaotic—job changes, illness, relocation, family upheaval—most people don't have the luxury of detailed budgeting. But they still need a mental model to make sense of their choices. The simplicity of five buckets means the system doesn't fracture under stress. It remains usable even when time is short and energy is depleted. You can glance at a paycheque or a bonus and think: "Have I covered Essentials? Have I invested in Growth? Is my Safety bucket sufficient? What can I allocate to Joy without compromising the rest? What's left in Overflow?" These are not abstract reflections—they are operational decisions, made sustainable by cognitive design.

It's worth noting that other attempts at simplifying budgeting have often swung too far in the opposite direction. The popular "50/30/20" rule, for example—50% needs, 30% wants, 20% savings—offers simplicity, but lacks nuance. It provides no space for the specific emotional or strategic roles money plays. Where does education go? Is it a want or a need? Where do you place redundancy planning, or investing in your children's future? What about overflow from bonuses or unexpected windfalls?

These frameworks collapse nuance into numerical symmetry. They're easy to remember but hard to live by—especially for people whose financial lives are complex or in transition.

The Five-Bucket model strikes a different balance. It is not a rule; it is a *lens*. It gives you structure, but not rigidity. Clarity, without compression. It respects your capacity for strategy while honouring your cognitive limitations. The model doesn't tell you what to do. It gives you a way to think—consistently, clearly, and in alignment with how your brain works best.

This cognitive foundation also makes the system more adaptable over time. As your income grows or contracts, as your goals shift, or as life throws surprises your way, the buckets remain stable. They are not tied to specific amounts or fixed percentages. They are functions. If Joy shrinks temporarily to accommodate a push in Growth or a reinforcement of Safety, the structure holds. If Overflow expands after a high-income month, it signals opportunity, not confusion. You aren't recalibrating dozens of categories—you're shifting weight within a sturdy frame.

The longevity of any financial system depends on whether people can return to it repeatedly without friction. Systems that overfit to ideal conditions rarely survive real life. The Five-Bucket model survives because it honours how people think under real conditions. Five is not a constraint—it's an enabling limit. It clears space for thought. It invites pattern recognition. It allows decision-making to evolve without becoming exhausting.

In behavioural economics, there is growing recognition that *choice architecture*—the way options are structured—shapes outcomes far more than we like to admit. Too few choices, and people feel constrained. Too many, and they become paralysed. The Five-Bucket system hits a psychological sweet spot. It reduces noise while preserving flexibility. It channels focus without demanding rigidity. It invites action without triggering fatigue.

There is elegance in systems that do less, better. The number five, in this context, is not arbitrary. It is a threshold—small enough to manage, rich enough to matter. In a culture obsessed with more—more data, more metrics, more control—this is a conscious act of restraint. A decision to optimise not for theoretical completeness, but for lived usability.

When a financial model aligns with how your brain naturally processes complexity, you don't need to outsource your clarity to apps or spreadsheets. You carry it with you. You think in buckets. You notice imbalances. You adapt intelligently. That is the power of five—not as a mnemonic trick, but as a framework calibrated to the human mind. Simplicity isn't a compromise. It's a strategy. And in personal finance, where sustainability beats perfection, that strategy is everything.

Fixed vs. Fluid: Structure Without Rigidity

A financial system that cannot bend will eventually break. This is the silent flaw at the core of most budgeting frameworks: they confuse structure with strictness, clarity with constraint. Their success depends on conditions remaining stable—steady income, predictable expenses, consistent behaviour. But life does not unfold on a spreadsheet. Income fluctuates. Priorities shift. Emergencies arise. Desires evolve. And any system that fails to accommodate this fluidity sets its users up not for financial empowerment, but for eventual disengagement. The strength of a personal budgeting framework lies not in how tightly it can hold, but in how flexibly it can adapt without losing its shape.

The Five-Bucket model is designed precisely around this insight. It offers a durable structure—a functional architecture of Essentials, Growth, Safety, Joy, and Overflow—without locking users into rigid formulas. There are no mandated percentages. No rules that collapse when life deviates from the mean. Instead, the model provides a consistent lens for understanding, adjusting, and aligning your financial behaviour across changing circumstances. *It is structured enough to create clarity, but fluid enough to accommodate reality.*

To appreciate the importance of this design, consider the lived experience of someone earning on commission or operating as a freelancer. Income may arrive in irregular bursts—£2,000 one month, £500 the next. In such a case, a fixed allocation model that prescribes exact figures or rigid proportions becomes unworkable. But the Five-Bucket approach remains relevant. Even when amounts vary, the structure remains stable: first, fund Essentials to keep life operational. Then, prioritise Safety to absorb volatility. After that, direct discretionary income toward Growth and Joy, letting Overflow serve as a signal for rebalancing. The proportions shift, but the framework holds. It provides coherence without control.

This is not merely useful for irregular earners. It matters equally for those moving through different life stages. A student in their early twenties will have vastly different priorities than a professional in mid-career or a retiree managing a fixed income. During early career phases, Essentials and Growth may dominate—paying rent, building skills, investing in education. Later, as earnings increase and risk tolerance changes, Safety may take precedence, or Joy may be given more space. At each point, the Five-Bucket structure remains intact, acting as a mirror that reflects evolving needs without imposing artificial constraints.

Contrast this with popular budgeting heuristics—like the "50/30/20 rule"—which advocate that 50% of income go to needs, 30% to wants, and 20% to savings. While appealing in their simplicity, these models assume a median financial profile. They are ill-suited to those with high fixed costs, significant debt, or non-traditional career paths. More importantly, they are static. If your rent jumps by 15%, or your income drops temporarily, the whole system begins to unravel. The Five-Bucket model avoids this brittleness by decoupling structure from uniformity. It does not care *how much* goes into each category. It cares *why*.

That "why" is critical. It invites users to design their financial lives based on function and context, not generic benchmarks. Take the example of a couple raising three young children on a modest household income. Their Essentials bucket may need to absorb a disproportionate share—covering childcare, groceries, and transportation. Joy may appear thinner for a season, but that's not a problem. It's a reflection of trade-offs. What matters is not the ratio, but the awareness that Joy hasn't disappeared—it's been right-sized for the current phase. And as children grow or incomes increase, the model allows for recalibration without any loss of integrity.

The same logic applies during life disruptions—redundancy, illness, divorce, or even rapid career growth. In a sudden downturn, a user may shift aggressively into Safety, cutting Joy to the bone and pausing Growth. When stability returns, those buckets can be rebalanced. In moments of windfall—a bonus, inheritance, or investment gain—Overflow becomes the holding space. It lets you pause and assess before allocating, reducing the risk of impulse and restoring intentionality. The system doesn't demand immediate compliance to rules. It gives you a place to *think* before you act.

This adaptability also enhances psychological resilience. Rigid systems often collapse under the weight of guilt. When users deviate from a strict plan—by overspending, skipping a savings transfer, or reallocating funds—they feel they've failed. The response is often disengagement: the spreadsheet is abandoned, the app deleted, the conversation avoided. But a flexible system fosters reflection rather than judgement. You didn't "break" your budget. You responded to new data. What matters now is how you reallocate going forward. This mindset is not only more sustainable—it's healthier.

In behavioural economics, this principle is reflected in the idea of *path dependency*. People are more likely to continue using systems that allow them to course-correct without resetting. The Five-Bucket model is intentionally path-dependent. It rewards engagement, not perfection. If one month's distribution was skewed, the next month offers an opportunity to adjust. No shame. No starting over. Just a continuation of strategic decision-making. This is financial planning as an evolving practice, not a pass/fail test.

The model's fluidity also proves advantageous in managing shared finances. For couples, families, or business partners, rigid structures often lead to conflict—one party adhering to "the plan," the other responding to changing needs. But a fluid model facilitates dialogue. It reframes disagreements: not "why did you overspend?" but "how are we balancing Growth and Joy this month?" Not "you're not saving enough," but "is our Safety bucket adequately funded for the risks we're carrying?" The structure becomes a shared language, not a point of contention.

Yet flexibility without anchors leads to chaos. The genius of the Five-Bucket model is that its structure is *functionally fixed*. The five categories never change. What varies is their content and weighting. This combination—fixed headings with variable application—mirrors successful frameworks in other disciplines. In design, it's called *constraint with freedom*. In language, it's grammar with creativity. In architecture, it's scaffolding with open floor plans. The strength of the model lies in giving people something reliable to push against, while still letting them shape it to their lives.

This structural integrity is particularly important for people rebuilding after financial hardship. For someone recovering from bankruptcy, starting over after divorce, or navigating job loss, a clear structure provides orientation. But rigidity at these moments is counterproductive. The Five-Bucket model allows people to start small—perhaps only funding Essentials and Safety at first—while keeping the broader map visible. The other buckets serve as aspirational placeholders. They remind users that their financial life has multiple dimensions, even if not all are currently resourced. That reminder is often more powerful than the numbers themselves.

It's also a myth that fluidity undermines accountability. In reality, people are more likely to track and reflect on systems that respect their lived experience. The buckets don't excuse poor decisions—they contextualise them. If your Joy bucket consistently crowds out Growth, that becomes a pattern worth investigating. If Overflow remains empty month after month, despite rising income, the model invites introspection. Not punitive scrutiny, but intelligent inquiry. It's accountability through alignment, not rigidity.

What emerges, then, is a system that stays usable through change. Whether you're earning six figures or living on a part-time wage, the model remains relevant. Whether your goals involve buying a home, travelling more, or retiring early, the framework adapts. Whether your life is calm, chaotic, or somewhere in between, the buckets give you a way to think clearly about your money without demanding that your life fit someone else's financial blueprint.

The brilliance of the Five-Bucket model is not that it solves every financial problem, but that it doesn't get in the way of solving them. It creates *just enough* structure to enable decision-making, reflection, and prioritisation—without ever pretending that one distribution, one month, or one model should apply forever. It gives you a financial system that stays legible, no matter how your life shifts. And that, in a world defined by change, is what durability truly looks like. Structure without rigidity. Fixed in form. Fluid in function. Designed for life.

Visualising Your Money Map

There is a profound clarity that emerges the moment you make the invisible visible. Most people live with a general sense of their finances—how much they earn, what their bills are, perhaps even how much they've saved. But rarely do they possess a coherent visual of where their money truly goes, how it functions within their life, and what it reveals about their values, fears, and aspirations. This is not due to negligence or lack of interest; it is the consequence of complexity. Income arrives from multiple sources, expenses recur unevenly, and spending often happens automatically, with little time for reflection. Without structure, the mental image of our financial life remains fragmented, abstract, or distorted. That's why a functional map—a simple yet meaningful sketch of your money flows—is not just helpful, but essential.

The Five-Bucket model lends itself to such a visualisation. Its power lies not merely in its conceptual clarity, but in its ability to become a living diagram of how your financial energy moves. By categorising money according to function—Essentials, Growth, Safety, Joy, and Overflow—you create a mental architecture that makes your money legible. And when that architecture is drawn out, literally mapped on paper or digitally charted, patterns emerge. These patterns are not just mathematical; they are behavioural, emotional, and strategic. *A money map reveals not just what you're doing with your money—but who you are becoming because of it.*

Begin with this question: if every pound you earned had a role, what job would it be doing right now? Take your current monthly income—net of taxes and deductions—and allocate it across the five buckets based on how you actually spend, not how you think you should. This is a diagnostic exercise, not a budgeting ideal. Whether your income is £2,000 or £20,000, the goal is to reflect, not optimise. If 80% of your income currently flows into Essentials, write that down. If Joy consumes 25% while Growth sits at zero, record that without judgement. The exercise only becomes useful when it is honest.

Next, sketch it. A pie chart, bar graph, or set of proportional boxes—use whatever format makes intuitive sense. Label each section with the bucket name and corresponding percentage or pound figure. What you are looking for is imbalance: not in the sense of moral failure, but in the context of intentional design. *Does your current distribution reflect the life you want—or the life you've defaulted into?*

For instance, someone in their early thirties with no dependents might discover that Essentials take up half their income, Joy 30%, Growth 10%, Safety 5%, and Overflow 5%. At first glance, this may appear reasonable—after all, the bills are paid and life feels enjoyable. But a closer inspection may reveal a fragile foundation. With Safety underfunded, a single medical bill or job disruption could derail the system. With Growth underweight, long-term optionality is quietly eroding. Meanwhile, Joy may be overactive—not out of hedonism, but as a substitute for burnout or dissatisfaction elsewhere. *Your money map is a mirror. It reflects not only your economics, but your psychology.*

This process becomes even more illuminating when repeated across different time frames. Create a monthly map, a quarterly map, and a projected annual map. Track how your allocations shift. Are you consistent in funding Growth and Safety, or do these get crowded out when large, unexpected Essentials arise? Do you overfund Joy during periods of stress and underfund it when life is stable? Does Overflow disappear entirely in some months, hinting at a lack of slack in your system? Each of these patterns points to potential areas of redesign—not in punitive ways, but in strategic ones.

Real-life examples help underscore this. Consider Ravi, a mid-career consultant with an annual income of £90,000. On paper, his financial life is sound: a stable job, no consumer debt, and regular pension contributions. But when he maps his money across the Five Buckets, he finds that 70% is absorbed by Essentials—mortgage, school fees, commuting, and food. Joy consumes another 20%—mostly travel and dining. That leaves just 5% each for Growth and Safety, with Overflow effectively nonexistent. Ravi isn't mismanaging his money. He is experiencing *functional crowding*. Too much of his income is locked into fixed, inflexible obligations, leaving little room to manoeuvre. The money map gives him a new question to work with: how can he restructure his Essentials—perhaps refinancing his mortgage, adjusting lifestyle expectations, or seeking remote work—to free capacity for long-term resilience?

Or take Anna, a self-employed graphic designer earning a variable income averaging £3,000 per month. She maps her actual flows and discovers something different. Essentials are just 40%, Joy 15%, Growth 10%, Safety 5%, and Overflow 30%. On the surface, this seems ideal—low overheads and plenty of slack. But a pattern emerges: the Overflow figure fluctuates dramatically month to month. When income is high, it spikes. When income dips, it disappears entirely. Anna realises her current system lacks *income smoothing*. Her Overflow isn't building intentional surplus—it's absorbing volatility. The money map gives her a strategic prompt: perhaps it's time to route part of Overflow automatically into Safety first, then determine discretionary spend from what remains. *Mapping reveals both the opportunity and the fragility.*

The power of this exercise lies in its recursive potential. You can revisit your money map each month, not as a form of micromanagement, but as a recalibration ritual. Small shifts can make large impacts. Moving 5% from Joy to Safety might not change your lifestyle dramatically, but it may double your buffer against disruption. Increasing Growth by just 3% per month compounds into significant life leverage over time—through skills, income, and autonomy. And if your Overflow begins to accumulate meaningfully, it becomes a strategic question: is this future Joy, future Safety, or the seed of a new Growth horizon?

But the map isn't only personal. It can be used relationally as well. Couples can map their shared and individual buckets to surface misalignments and values-based differences. A partner who allocates heavily toward Joy may not be irresponsible—they may be expressing a deep-seated philosophy of presence or generosity. A partner who prioritises Safety may not be fearful—they may be carrying the psychological load of prior instability. The Five-Bucket map becomes not just a financial tool, but a medium for mutual understanding. *It externalises what is often left unsaid.*

Equally, for financial planners, coaches, or therapists, the money map offers a more human diagnostic than line-item budgets. Rather than asking clients to categorise expenses in excruciating detail, they can invite clients to map functions. Where is the money doing the work of security, aspiration, expression, stability, or expansion? What is being underfed? What is being overfed? This reframing creates more powerful, less shame-inducing conversations. It connects financial behaviour to life design.

What distinguishes this tool is its emphasis on intention over perfection. The point is not to draw a flawless map, but to make a visible claim on your financial landscape. The process itself triggers awareness. And awareness leads to design. If your current flows don't reflect your priorities, you can change them—not overnight, but iteratively. If your current allocations are shaped by fear, inertia, or assumption, you can surface those patterns and start asking better questions. The money map is not a judgement. It's a compass. And the more you consult it, the more you begin to move with clarity, not just discipline.

Ultimately, the Five-Bucket money map offers something few financial tools do: *a holistic, non-punitive snapshot of financial function anchored in personal agency*. It requires no special software, no precision tracking, and no moralising. It simply asks you to see. To draw the real shape of your money, with honesty and curiosity. To interpret the contours not as constraints, but as choices. And then, to begin adjusting the flow—not toward perfection, but toward alignment. Over time, this becomes more than an exercise. It becomes a habit of consciousness. A way to ensure that your money is not just spent or saved, but *understood*.

Chapter 3
Essentials—Build the Floor, Not the Cage

Every financial system, however sophisticated, rests on a deceptively simple question: what do you truly need? Its apparent simplicity belies the depth of its consequences, reaching into every facet of our economic lives. Traditional budgets treat "essentials"—rent, utilities, groceries, transport—as immutable line items. They are accepted unquestioningly, often considered beyond debate. Yet one must ask: have we quietly inflated the notion of essentials—not through necessity, but assumption? Might the foundation we believe sustains us actually constrain us?

In contemporary consumer cultures, it is all too easy to conflate obligations with needs. A high-end phone plan, a gym membership untouched for months, premium groceries, streaming subscriptions—all can migrate into the "essential" column without scrutiny. We tell ourselves these are indispensable, prudent even. But the expansion of the essential category is rarely a reflection of weakness; it is the product of a culture that markets comfort as necessity, convenience as duty, and status as utility. To build a financial system anchored in reality, we must distinguish what sustains life from what merely sustains lifestyle.

This chapter begins by interrogating the assumption that fixed costs are inherently non-discretionary. While shelter, food, and energy access are genuinely non-negotiable, many purported essentials are choices masquerading as mandates. Even within these core domains, costs vary widely. A family renting a two-bedroom flat in Manchester may pay three times what a couple in rural Wales pays on their mortgage, yet both would classify housing as essential. The question is not whether housing is necessary, but whether the form we occupy has been consciously chosen or unconsciously inherited.

Transport offers a similar illustration. Car ownership is often treated as a given, even in urban areas with robust public transit, or where remote work has reduced commuting. For many, a car conveys autonomy, safety, or identity. Yet what begins as a tool frequently hardens into a fixture: monthly payments, insurance, fuel, and maintenance lock away resources that could otherwise flow to Growth, Safety, or Joy. The rigidity of these "fixed" costs creates fragility. A system is only as resilient as its least flexible component.

Fragility remains invisible while income flows steadily; inefficiencies feel tolerable until circumstances shift. Job loss, illness, rent increases, or broader economic turbulence can transform comfort into liability overnight. In this context, the true measure of an essential is not habitual use, but sustainability under pressure. Resilience is less about austerity than agility. And agility begins with redefining the boundary of what we consider foundational.

This is not an argument for deprivation. The goal is not asceticism but alignment: a durable floor that protects rather than confines. Achieving this requires moving from passive budgeting to active design. Not merely: "Can I afford this rent?" but: "What cost does this rent impose across Growth, Safety, Joy?" Not simply: "Do I need a car?" but: "What role does this vehicle play in the life I want to live?" These are not bookkeeping questions—they are design questions.

To make such distinctions concrete, the chapter introduces a framework for evaluating Essentials through thresholds: sufficient, sustainable, and excessive. Housing evaluation involves square footage, location premiums, and ownership versus rental trade-offs. Food assessment incorporates emotional and cultural drivers behind groceries, dining out, and convenience purchases. Utilities and connectivity are analysed through the lens of actual utility versus perceived comfort.

We also address anchoring—the psychological stickiness of early choices. The first flat you rented, the baseline grocery habit, the default transport mode: these establish reference points persisting long after context changes. Anchoring influences both expenditure and perception of what should be spent. A person who once lived alone in a city-centre flat may struggle to consider shared housing or suburban relocation, even if doing so could release thousands annually. The objective is awareness, not moralisation. Essentials deserve periodic reevaluation, not because one must downgrade, but because life may have outgrown the assumptions on which those costs were built.

Emotional factors are inseparable from this calculus. Downsizing a flat or replacing a car may make sense on paper, but choices entangled with identity, comfort, and social perception rarely yield to spreadsheets alone. This chapter explores the emotional architecture of Essentials: what your home communicates, what your car permits you to signal or escape from, and what trade-offs have been avoided due to comparison, family pressure, or fear of appearing "less than." The goal is not to strip Essentials bare, but to strip them of illusion, revealing their true role in your financial ecosystem.

A practical illustration: Amina and David, a dual-income couple in a high-rent area, made the bold choice to downsize their flat and replace a second car with a hybrid work schedule and bicycle. Their income was rising, yet Essentials consumed 75 per cent of earnings, starving Growth, Joy, and Overflow. The adjustment was challenging—friction, ego, and long-avoided conversations—but within six months, they had tripled their Safety fund, reactivated stalled savings goals, and discovered a daily rhythm that felt lighter, not diminished. They did not cut back—they stepped back. What they found was not scarcity, but space.

By chapter's end, readers will have the tools to conduct an Essential audit—not through line-item excision, but through role-based questioning. They will map their current essentials, interrogate assumptions, and reallocate with clarity. More importantly, they will come to see Essentials as design choices, not inherited mandates. A well-crafted financial floor does more than sustain; it protects, supports, adapts, and leaves room to breathe. It does not merely hold you up—it helps you rise.

Redefining Needs vs. Obligations

The distinction between a need and an obligation is rarely interrogated with the seriousness it deserves. For most households, the monthly budget begins with a column of expenses labelled "fixed"—rent or mortgage, utilities, broadband, insurance, car payments, mobile contracts, subscriptions. These line items are rarely questioned, much less challenged. They are pencilled in as non-negotiables, long before any discussion of savings, joy, or aspiration is allowed to begin. The logic is simple: if it recurs, if it's hard to cancel, or if it has a bill attached, it must be a need. But this logic is dangerously flawed. *Many obligations masquerade as needs not because they are essential to life, but because they have become habitual, expected, or socially normalised.*

Cultural conditioning plays a more powerful role in our perception of necessity than we like to admit. Consider the rapid normalisation of smartphones: in less than two decades, mobile connectivity has gone from luxury to baseline infrastructure. Today, it's not unusual to see people earning less than £25,000 a year financing £1,000 phones on multi-year contracts. The expense is justified as an essential—connectivity for work, safety, navigation, communication. All true, to an extent. But buried within that justification is a conflation of *function* and *form*. Connectivity may be essential; the latest flagship device is not. Yet the cost is treated the same.

This inflation of the "essentials" category is not limited to technology. Housing is another prime example. The number of bedrooms, postcode, access to amenities, interior finishes—each factor creeps into the decision-making process as though it were a basic requirement. But shelter, while a universal need, is not synonymous with comfort, space, or prestige. There is a measurable difference between safe housing and lifestyle housing. The former offers security and functionality; the latter offers signalling, convenience, and often, emotional validation. *When our essentials are shaped by lifestyle aspirations rather than life-supporting functions, the budget ceases to reflect financial reality and begins to reflect social theatre.*

To understand how this happens, we must consider the silent pressures embedded in modern living. Cultural anthropology tells us that needs are never defined in isolation—they are constructed within a web of social reference points. Your definition of "enough" is calibrated, often unconsciously, against your peer group, your upbringing, and the ambient narratives you absorb from media, advertising, and social platforms. The idea that a young professional should live alone, in a city-centre flat, furnished tastefully, with high-speed broadband and a streaming bundle, feels normal only because the culture has packaged it as a milestone. It has very little to do with survival or opportunity. And yet, such arrangements routinely consume over 60% of take-home pay among urban earners under 35. *At that level of overhead, the problem is not lack of income—it's misallocated obligation.*

Fixed costs are dangerous precisely because they are perceived as permanent. Once established, they resist scrutiny. They're paid by direct debit, structured into contracts, and baked into our mental models of daily life. But permanence is not the same as necessity. A person paying £1,800 a month in rent may feel trapped, but they are often not imprisoned by the market—they are imprisoned by their perception of what's non-negotiable. The solution isn't always to move; sometimes, it's to re-examine what trade-offs you're unwilling to consider. Why is a 30-minute commute off-limits? Why is a house-share beneath your dignity? Why is a modest kitchen a source of shame? These questions are uncomfortable because they puncture the illusion of fixedness. *Once you realise your "needs" are partly choices, the burden of financial immobility begins to lighten—but so too does your margin for excuse.*

Even subscriptions—seemingly minor—demonstrate this slippage between obligation and need. A Netflix plan here, a fitness app there, a cloud storage service, a meal kit. Each item is inexpensive in isolation, easy to justify, and frictionless to sustain. Collectively, they build a monthly scaffold of assumed necessity that few ever dismantle. Most people couldn't even list all their recurring payments without checking their statements. The danger isn't just financial; it's cognitive. *Every false need you accept narrows your field of vision and restricts your capacity for strategic choice.*

This is where redefinition becomes not only practical, but philosophical. To redefine a need is to ask, "What do I require to live with safety, dignity, and agency?" Not comfort, not consistency, not image—*agency*. The ability to adapt, to pivot, to recover from shock. A budget anchored in true needs creates space—space for resilience, for growth, for missteps. A budget inflated with obligations creates rigidity. One lost income stream, one medical bill, one relocation—and the entire structure begins to buckle. This isn't theory. It's observable in data from households that live paycheck to paycheck across income levels. Not all financial stress comes from scarcity. Much of it comes from structural overcommitment based on misidentified needs.

Crucially, the process of redefining isn't binary. You don't need to cut your life down to bare bones. Rather, you need to *surface assumptions*—to interrogate each fixed cost not with guilt, but with clarity. Is this expenditure still serving me? Does it reflect my current life stage, goals, and values? Could I meet the same function—safety, nourishment, transport, connectivity—at a lower cost without meaningful loss of quality? These are not trivial questions. They require a mindset shift from consumption to design.

Consider the following illustrative case. Two professionals, both earning £60,000 annually, live in the same city. One allocates £2,000 per month to housing, utilities, car finance, and lifestyle subscriptions. The other limits these categories to £1,200 by choosing a less central flat, a used car, and fewer digital services. The first has no room to invest, save, or absorb shocks. The second funds a pension, maintains a Safety fund, and takes annual holidays. On paper, both appear to have stable lives. But only one has financial *mobility*. The other is an economic hostage to their own defaults. *This divergence is not about income—it's about which costs were allowed to calcify into the "need" category without interrogation.*

This analysis is not an argument for austerity. It is a framework for autonomy. Reducing unnecessary obligations does not mean reducing quality of life—it often means reclaiming it. Less rent might mean more travel. Less car might mean more walking, more community, less stress. Fewer subscriptions might mean more intentional use of time. The aim is not to shrink your life but to *sharpen its contours*. To direct your resources with purpose, not inertia.

The practical application of this idea is simple but profound: conduct a "needs audit." List your fixed costs and ask, for each, "Is this essential for life or just embedded in habit?" Don't ask, "Can I afford it?" Ask, "Does it expand or restrict my capacity to choose?" True essentials provide leverage. False needs deplete it.

This subchapter lays the intellectual foundation for rebuilding the Essentials bucket with clarity. As you read further into this chapter, you'll encounter frameworks for assessing rent, transport, food, and utilities through a new lens—not the lens of tradition or social expectation, but of strategic sufficiency. The result is not minimalism. It's *precision*. Not just lower expenses, but better ones. Not fewer comforts, but fewer traps. Because when you stop mistaking obligations for needs, what remains is not just a leaner budget—it's a freer life.

Rent, Food, Utilities: The Right Thresholds

There's an often-overlooked truth hiding behind most personal budgets: the biggest financial decisions people make are not made monthly, but structurally. Long before a person sets out to track spending or set a savings target, their recurring costs—especially rent, food, and utilities—have already defined the landscape in which all other money decisions must unfold. These categories are frequently labelled as "non-negotiables" or "essentials," but that terminology conceals a crucial distinction: not all recurring costs are inevitable, and not all 'needs' are equal. What most budgets mistakenly present as fixed and immovable are, in reality, saturated with hidden assumptions, cultural expectations, and lifestyle drift.

The essential isn't what you need to survive—it's what you need to sustain a life that makes sense for your values and circumstances. This is a nuanced threshold, not a formula. And until that line is drawn with deliberation, these recurring costs risk becoming silent saboteurs of long-term financial mobility.

Let's begin with rent, the largest single expense for most households. Conventional advice often suggests allocating no more than 30% of gross income to housing. Yet this rule of thumb, originating from mid-20th century U.S. housing policy rather than behavioural economics, lacks relevance in many modern contexts. In global cities and high-cost metros, 30% is frequently unattainable, while in lower-cost regions, people may spend far less but still feel financially constrained. The issue isn't strictly percentage—it's proportion and priority. Rent becomes a problem not when it exceeds a certain ratio, but when it limits the capacity to fund other essential functions: saving, investing, or absorbing life's inevitable variability.

A better approach begins with evaluating housing through the lens of *flexibility-to-sacrifice ratio*. For example, paying £1,200 per month for a studio flat that shortens your commute and reduces your transport needs may actually represent better value than paying £900 for a flat that requires a car, fuel, and two hours of daily travel. Similarly, shared housing or co-living arrangements, long stigmatised as student-like compromises, can be reclaimed as deliberate strategies for mobility, whether geographic, financial, or personal.

The same logic applies to food, another cost often treated as static. Grocery bills and dining habits are among the most culturally coded and psychologically charged aspects of spending. The language around food—organic, artisanal, clean, cheap, healthy—often reflects identity more than necessity. While nutritional adequacy has a clear baseline, what one person sees as a daily requirement, another might view as discretionary. Meal delivery, barista-grade coffee, farmers' markets, takeaway habits—all blur the line between nourishment and indulgence. To shrink food spending without deprivation, the key is pattern recalibration, not restriction. Batch cooking, meal planning, and reducing 'decision points' (those daily "what should I eat?" moments) can preserve satisfaction while lowering cost and cognitive load.

Utilities, meanwhile, are rarely interrogated, despite being a persistent site of silent inflation. Broadband, for instance, is often bundled with unnecessary channels or premium plans. Energy tariffs go unreviewed. Smartphone plans renew with inertia. In most households, utilities reflect legacy decisions—packages selected years ago and left untouched. There is room here not just for switching providers or reducing use, but for rethinking what constitutes "enough." Do you need ultrafast speeds for a household of two? Is a 24/7 hot water supply essential, or a holdover from a time when energy was cheap and environmental impact negligible?

What unites rent, food, and utilities under the "Essentials" banner is their foundational nature: these are the inputs that keep life operational. But *essential does not mean untouchable.* When you see these categories as settings to be calibrated—rather than ceilings to be accepted—you reclaim agency over your cost base. That's the real shift: moving from seeing fixed costs as dictated by the world to seeing them as *aligned with your world.*

More fundamentally, this reframing opens space for proportionality. Rather than trying to cut everything evenly or shave pennies off already-lean areas, individuals can make asymmetric adjustments with asymmetric gains. A £150 rent reduction often yields more financial room than eliminating every takeaway coffee in a month. Shrinking the essentials bucket without sacrifice is about surgical edits, not blanket austerity.

This is particularly relevant in life transitions. Whether it's moving cities, changing jobs, or starting a family, many assume their cost structure must scale upward. But the essentials bucket should not inflate automatically with age, income, or status. If anything, it should *decelerate* over time as experience refines what truly adds value. A person in their thirties may discover that living with less space, but more proximity to nature or community, offers more satisfaction than upgrading to a detached house with a longer commute.

Of course, there are non-negotiables: rent must be paid, food must be eaten, energy must run. But the *how, where,* and *how much* remain surprisingly pliable. The right threshold is not an average or an algorithm—it's a deliberate negotiation between autonomy and sufficiency, between freedom and infrastructure. This is why Essentials are not a cage to be endured, but a floor to be examined, tested, and made efficient.

Ultimately, the true test of whether something belongs in this bucket is *substitutability*. If a particular housing setup, meal plan, or utility bundle can be restructured without undermining your baseline functioning, then the current version may not be essential—it may just be familiar. Familiarity, while comfortable, often leads to stagnation. Challenging it, even once a year, yields better calibration and intentionality.

Essentials should support your life, not dominate it. And the litmus test for sustainability isn't how normal the expense feels—but how well it fits your broader financial architecture. Rent, food, and utilities can either serve as stable scaffolding for growth or as slow leaks that erode potential. Knowing the difference starts with asking better questions and resisting the passivity embedded in fixed-cost assumptions. Shrinking this bucket without sacrifice is less about belt-tightening and more about sight-lifting—an elevated view of what you need, what you've accepted, and what you're ready to rethink.

Anchoring vs. Agility in Housing and Transport

There's a quiet paradox at the heart of modern personal finance: many people work harder, earn more, and still feel cornered by their cost of living. Not extravagance, not luxury—just the monthly baseline. And when we investigate why, the answer tends to sit in two immovable pillars: rent and transport. These aren't mere expenses; they're architectural decisions. They frame the space within which all other financial choices must operate. Once locked in, they act as anchors—setting the depth of your fixed costs, the pace of your lifestyle, and the range of your options. And unlike discretionary spending, they can't be casually trimmed or renegotiated mid-month. This makes them deceptively powerful—and therefore, deserving of far greater scrutiny than most people apply.

The real problem is not that housing or transport are expensive—though they often are—but that the way we approach them is riddled with outdated assumptions. People still tend to treat location and mobility as life constants rather than levers. Rent is dictated by zip code; transport by commute; both by social defaults inherited from earlier decades. But modern work, urban design, and technology have quietly upended those scripts. You no longer need to live in a city centre to access opportunity, nor do you need a car to participate in modern life. Yet budgeting frameworks—and often even financial advice—remain anchored in the idea that these are fixed, even sacred, categories of spending.

But they're not. They're strategic trade-offs. And the more deliberately we treat them, the more space we reclaim in the rest of our financial lives.

Let's begin with housing. When people choose where to live, they're often making more than just a cost decision—they're choosing proximity, identity, and perceived security. The appeal of a nicer flat, a better postcode, or an extra bedroom is rarely about square footage alone. It's about lifestyle signalling. A certain address may feel like it confirms progress; a certain neighbourhood may feel safer or more adult. The result? People regularly commit 35%–50% of their net income to rent, mortgage, council tax, and utilities bundled into a housing decision that looked logical on paper—but quietly chokes cash flow month after month.

The mental model here needs updating. Housing shouldn't be seen solely as an "anchor" that grounds you. It should also be assessed as a *platform*—a base from which other life functions are either enabled or constrained. For example, paying more to live in walkable proximity to work, school, or childcare may yield daily time dividends and reduce other categories of spending. But if the cost of that choice eats into savings, emergency funds, or career flexibility, the net effect may be negative. Conversely, relocating to a lower-cost area with remote work viability may reduce prestige but increase life options—financial, geographic, even psychological. The question isn't "Can I afford this rent?" It's *"What does this rent cost me elsewhere?"*

The same logic applies, often more dramatically, in the domain of transport. Few financial commitments are as misleadingly stable as car ownership. The monthly payment looks fixed—but the real cost is layered: fuel, insurance, maintenance, depreciation, registration, repairs, and, increasingly, parking or congestion charges. In the UK, the average cost of owning and operating a car is estimated to exceed £3,000 per year, with little correlation to actual utility for many urban residents. And yet the car remains one of the most culturally defended 'essentials'—an emblem of freedom and status, even in contexts where it functions more as a liability.

Here's the shift: *mobility is not the same as ownership.* Access to reliable transport need not mean a long-term vehicle lease or finance agreement. For increasing numbers of people, especially in well-connected urban areas, alternatives now outperform ownership on both cost and convenience: car-sharing platforms, cycling infrastructure, ride-hailing, public transport subscriptions, even walking. But opting out of car ownership still feels socially or emotionally radical for many, particularly those raised in car-centric environments. That discomfort is not about function—it's about narrative. Which means the real work is not in spreadsheets, but in mindset.

What complicates both rent and transport is that they're often bundled with identity. People fear that downsizing or going car-free will signal regression, not prudence. But the fear is usually imagined. There is no virtue in carrying a housing cost that inhibits your ability to save, invest, or explore career changes. There is no badge for spending £400 monthly on a vehicle that mostly sits idle. These are not markers of adulthood—they're constraints, if chosen without thought.

Anchoring refers to the cognitive bias that leads people to rely heavily on the first piece of information they receive when making decisions. In housing and transport, anchoring manifests in habits like searching for flats based on your last salary level, choosing your next car based on the cost of your current one, or maintaining a living standard that matched a previous lifestyle—but no longer fits current goals. These defaults compound. Each renewal cycle—be it a lease, a car finance agreement, or an annual insurance policy—becomes an opportunity either to entrench a suboptimal commitment or to re-anchor consciously.

And yet, for all the economic and psychological baggage tied up in these choices, the solution is not austerity—it's agility. A flexible approach to housing and transport doesn't mean instability. It means *designing these categories to bend with your life, not break it.* This includes:

- Renting with exit flexibility rather than locking into multi-year contracts when life is in flux
- Choosing locations based on function, not prestige, particularly if remote or hybrid work is viable
- Treating cars as tools, not trophies—replacing ownership with access when appropriate
- Revisiting large financial anchors at least annually, not just when forced to by crisis

This is not about minimalism for its own sake. It's about building in *optionality*. When 40%–60% of your net income is bound up in housing and transport, there's limited room to manoeuvre. But when those same needs are met with strategic frugality and thoughtful design, you create structural breathing space for growth. That breathing space is what allows you to respond to opportunity, handle disruption, or simply *rest without debt*.

A final point worth stressing: agility is context-sensitive. A single parent with school-bound children faces different constraints than a digital nomad in their twenties. But in both cases, agility is not about geography—it's about intention. It's the difference between living where you are because it's default, versus living there because it works. The latter makes room for clarity, savings, creativity—even joy. The former just eats your margin.

What housing and transport ultimately ask us to confront is *how much infrastructure your life truly requires*. Anchors can stabilise—but only when consciously placed. Otherwise, they simply drag. Financial flexibility is not found in budgeting apps or spreadsheets; it begins upstream, in the structural costs that shape every downstream decision. The goal is not to eliminate anchors, but to choose ones that empower movement—physical, financial, and psychological. Anything else is just sinking in place.

Case Study: The Couple Who Downsized to Expand

Most financial transformations don't begin with a windfall. They begin with a decision that feels, at first, like a step backwards. This is the story of Matthew and Priya—two professionals in their late thirties living in Manchester—who discovered that the most liberating move in their financial lives wasn't earning more, investing smarter, or side-hustling harder. It was the quiet, deeply intentional act of reimagining what they truly needed from their home. In doing so, they cut their fixed costs in half and redirected the difference not just into savings, but into a dramatically more fulfilling life.

At the outset, Matthew and Priya's story looked familiar: a dual-income couple with steady but unremarkable salaries—he worked in product design for a regional software firm, she was a physiotherapist for the NHS. They lived in a spacious two-bedroom flat in the city's Northern Quarter, paying £1,700 per month in rent, plus another £400 in associated bills. Their combined income after tax came to just under £5,500 monthly. On paper, they were comfortably middle class. In practice, their monthly budget felt perpetually tight.

They weren't extravagant spenders. They didn't travel often, didn't own a car, and rarely ate out. But between rent, council tax, broadband, groceries, and student loan repayments, over 70% of their take-home income was spoken for before they even considered discretionary spending or savings. What began as mild financial friction became chronic stress during the pandemic, when Priya's work hours were reduced and Matthew's job security wavered. The flat they once saw as a marker of their professional progress started to feel like a gilded trap.

The turning point came one rainy Thursday evening over dinner, when a friend casually mentioned that she'd cut her living expenses by moving to a smaller unit outside the city centre. "It's not glamorous," she had laughed, "but I'm sleeping better knowing I'm not paying for 300 square feet of storage I never use." The comment lodged in Priya's mind. That night, she pulled up a rental map and filtered for one-bedroom properties in neighbourhoods they'd previously written off as "transitional." What she found surprised her—not just in price, but in potential.

A week later, they toured a bright, modest one-bedroom flat in Sale, about 25 minutes from the city by tram. It was newly renovated, near a green space, and walking distance from a high street with the basics. Rent: £925 a month. Council tax and utilities would come in lower as well. The initial reaction was mixed—downsizing felt regressive, almost punitive. But the spreadsheet told a different story. By moving, they would free up over £800 per month. That's

£9,600 annually—more than either of them had ever saved in a year.

What followed wasn't just a change of address. It was a reframing of identity. Matthew worried about feeling "less professional" without the cachet of a city address. Priya feared their families would see it as financial failure. But both began to interrogate those fears. What was the purpose of their housing if not to support the rest of their lives? Why continue living in a space that restricted every other dimension of mobility—professional, emotional, and financial?

Within three months, they made the move. The shift was immediate. The smaller space forced them to sell or donate excess belongings, simplifying their living environment. Their commute increased slightly but was offset by better work-from-home arrangements negotiated with their employers. Most critically, they now had margin—financial breathing room they hadn't known in years. Within the first year, they paid off Matthew's lingering credit card balance, created a six-month emergency fund, and began investing into ISAs for long-term growth.

But the gains weren't only numeric. The psychological shift was profound. *They no longer felt trapped by their lifestyle.* That sense of agency translated into other areas of life. Priya enrolled in a postgraduate certification programme, partially funded by their surplus. Matthew took a sabbatical three months later to explore a business idea. Neither could have imagined making such moves in their old budget structure. Downsizing their space expanded their life.

Their story illustrates a concept that's easily discussed but rarely lived: *essentials are defined by purpose, not permanence.* Housing isn't essential because it's expensive. It's essential because it protects your ability to think, rest, and operate in the world. But when the cost of that protection exceeds its utility—when it starts to consume the very margin it's meant to create—it becomes counterproductive.

Matthew and Priya also show that sacrifice isn't the right lens. They didn't lose quality of life. They gained sovereignty over it. The new flat didn't have a second bedroom, but it had fewer distractions. It didn't have high ceilings, but it had low stress. Their social life shifted from impromptu city drinks to intentional gatherings at friends' homes. Their weekends no longer revolved around compensating for weekday exhaustion. They weren't "cutting back"—they were cutting *out* friction.

Critics might argue this is only possible for child-free couples or people without complex care obligations. But the principle remains adaptable: it's not about moving to the suburbs, it's about moving away from inertia. For others, the trade-off might involve moving into a house-share temporarily, leveraging intergenerational housing, or redesigning floor plans in multi-use spaces. What matters is that the choice is *functional,* not performative.

This case study also exposes a deeper tension in modern budgeting philosophy: most people are conditioned to optimise the margins of their spending—subscriptions, groceries, entertainment—while leaving the largest buckets unquestioned. Rent and transport are treated as fixed points, when in fact they are the greatest levers. The cultural reluctance to address them directly stems from status anxiety, habit, and a fear of appearing as though one is "moving backwards." But financial progress doesn't always look like expansion. Sometimes it looks like compression—creating tighter, more elegant systems that free up energy and intention elsewhere.

To put it more bluntly: what's the point of living in a premium property if you're too tired, anxious, or overworked to enjoy it?

Matthew and Priya's journey wasn't about frugality. It was about fit. They designed a home that served the life they wanted, not the lifestyle they assumed they should project. That kind of design thinking—rooted in flexibility, clarity, and trade-off analysis—is far more valuable than any budget template. It creates a system where *money is a tool, not a trap*.

If there's a lesson to draw from their story, it's this: your "essentials" don't define your limits. They define your launchpad. And if that pad is consuming more fuel than it provides, the answer isn't to work harder. It's to redesign it. With less surface area, they found more room to move. And that, ultimately, is the kind of wealth most worth pursuing.

Chapter 4
Growth—Where Wealth Is Built

Most people assume that wealth begins with having more money. In reality, it begins with how one deploys even a small surplus. Growth is not a privilege reserved for the already affluent—it is the mechanism through which anyone can build wealth. Yet much of personal finance frames growth too narrowly, reducing it to market returns, interest rates, or the quest for the lowest-fee platform. While such details matter, they obscure a more fundamental truth: growth is not merely an account type. It is a mindset. It is the deliberate transformation of today's resources into tomorrow's possibilities, regardless of how modest those resources may seem.

Adopting a growth-oriented mindset requires seeing money not only as a medium of consumption or preservation, but as a vehicle for multiplication. Crucially, this mental shift is accessible at any income level. For those with lower or irregular earnings, it can be especially potent, because the margin between stagnation and mobility is narrower, and small decisions have outsized impact. The myth that one must "get ahead" before pursuing growth is both widespread and corrosive. In fact, growth is often a prerequisite for financial security, not merely a consequence of it.

Within the Five-Bucket framework, Growth spans three interrelated domains: earning capacity, financial capital, and ownership. Each serves as a distinct engine. Human capital—the knowledge and skills one possesses—fuels income potential. Financial investments—stocks, bonds, business ventures—generate compounding returns. Ownership—of property, intellectual property, or infrastructure—anchors long-term stability and optionality. Together, these streams form a lattice capable of supporting upward mobility over a lifetime, provided it is built consciously.

Consider a delivery driver with an erratic schedule and modest savings. They might assume that investing in growth is a luxury beyond their reach. Yet even small, consistent contributions—£25 weekly into an index fund—constitute financial growth. Spending £150 on a course that enhances employability is another form. Or using surplus cash to launch a small side venture or acquire essential tools for freelance work. The forms differ, but the principle is constant: any deliberate allocation of money that expands future earning, ownership, or compounding potential qualifies as growth. Intentionality, not scale, is key.

Paradoxically, the modern economy offers unprecedented low-cost, high-upside growth opportunities, yet many treat surplus income as disposable. Lifestyle creep quietly diverts raises, bonuses, or windfalls into immediate consumption rather than strategic deployment. Sustainable growth does not require denying comfort or joy—it requires pre-allocating surplus toward compounding outcomes. The difference between an extra £100 spent on shoes versus invested in a course, emergency fund, or entrepreneurial idea illustrates this principle.

This chapter focuses on practical growth architecture, guiding the allocation of the Growth bucket across three categories: Learning (skills, credentials, personal development), Earning (business ventures, entrepreneurial efforts, work-optimised assets), and Ownership (financial and tangible capital with return potential). While these categories overlap, they serve as lenses to assess whether resources are positioned to expand freedom, resilience, and earning potential over time.

Growth is not merely forward motion—it is purposeful direction. One individual may channel Growth toward a career pivot, another toward property acquisition, another toward early retirement investments. Wealth is subjective, dependent on life stage, personality, and ambition. No single benchmark dictates the "correct" allocation. Yet behavioural heuristics offer guidance: allocating roughly 15–25 per cent of post-essential surplus to growth (before Joy and Overflow allocations) often produces meaningful long-term results, even if done incrementally.

Equally vital is intentionality. Allocations must be tracked and reviewed; growth does not flourish by chance. It is cultivated, requiring a willingness to confront inertia, to divert energy from routine consumption toward uncertain—but high-leverage—investments. This process can feel uncomfortable precisely because it challenges familiar patterns. Growth demands a deliberate break from the predictability of recurring expenses toward strategic effort.

To visualise this, imagine two individuals with identical incomes and savings rates. One channels surplus into short-term comforts; the other invests in skill-building, index funds, or a nascent entrepreneurial venture. Five years on, their financial trajectories diverge markedly; ten years on, they are scarcely comparable. The difference lies not in luck or innate talent, but in design. One system preserves inputs; the other generates outputs.

This chapter emphasises building upward through precision rather than perfection. It highlights high-leverage applications of limited capital, treating each allocation as a calculated investment in future optionality. Readers will encounter frameworks to evaluate growth aligned with life stage and personal priorities, supported by practical scenarios that shift financial planning from reactive to proactive.

Ultimately, growth is not a luxury reserved for the wealthy. It is the pathway by which ordinary people create extraordinary futures. A side project becomes a career. A certification becomes a new income stream. A single share becomes a first step on the ownership ladder. The quiet discipline of deliberate allocation transforms into long-term financial sovereignty.

The question is not whether growth is possible—it is whether you are intentionally building for it. This chapter serves as both a prompt and a blueprint. You do not need a larger income to begin. You need alignment: ensuring your money works on behalf of your future. The Growth bucket exists to create that alignment—deliberately, sustainably, and intelligently. The sooner you fill it with intention, the sooner it begins to work for you.

The Investment Mindset for Any Income

It is a dangerous misconception that investment is a privilege of the affluent. This notion—quietly embedded in the language of finance, reinforced by media imagery, and sustained by the gatekeeping of jargon—has kept millions from participating in the very process that enables upward mobility. At its core, investment is not a financial product. It is a way of thinking about money: *every pound has potential, and your task is to assign it a purpose that grows*. Once this mindset is understood—deeply, behaviourally—it becomes clear that investing is not something you wait to do after you "have enough." It is what you do in order to have enough.

For most, the term "investment" conjures images of equity markets, index funds, or property portfolios. While these are valid growth tools, they represent only a sliver of the full landscape. The broader and more practical definition—especially for those operating on modest or volatile incomes—is that *investment is any use of money that increases your future capacity, income, autonomy, or resilience*. In this light, the purchase of a second-hand laptop to start freelance work is an investment. So is a £20 online course that unlocks new job qualifications. So is spending time and transport money to attend a local business network. Investment is not what the bank labels it; it's what creates compound returns over time—financial or otherwise.

For low- and middle-income earners, embracing this expansive view of investing is not just empowering; it is essential. When margins are tight, each unit of surplus has disproportionate importance. Every discretionary pound is a fork in the road: it can reinforce your current trajectory or create the possibility of a different one. The old advice—

save diligently, budget sensibly, and one day you may invest—fails under modern conditions. Inflation eats savings faster than interest can preserve them, and wages rarely outpace the cost of stability. In contrast, investment—even in its smallest, most humble form—provides leverage. It multiplies future options in a way that saving alone does not.

This distinction between saving and investing is not semantic. It is functional. Saving preserves. Investment produces. A jar of rice in a cupboard and a handful of rice in fertile soil serve different ends. For those with limited cash flow, the challenge is to identify which small acts of planting are available—and to execute them with intention.

Consider the story of Amina, a part-time teaching assistant earning just above minimum wage in Birmingham. For years, she believed that investing wasn't for her. Her priority was security: ensuring rent, food, and utilities were covered each month, with the occasional treat or holiday escape. When she received a modest inheritance of £2,000 following a distant relative's passing, her instinct was to keep it in a high-interest savings account. But after a brief conversation with a mentor, she shifted course. £300 went to buy a refurbished camera. Another £200 paid for an online certification in event photography. She used £100 to market herself locally. Within six months, weekend photo gigs added an average of £150 to her monthly income. Within a year, she was making more from photography than her school job. The initial capital outlay was small, but the mindset shift was tectonic. She began seeing money as a tool, not just a safety net.

It would be misleading to suggest that everyone's path is so straightforward. Risk is real. Timing matters. Not all bets pay off. But that is precisely why investment requires a mindset—not just a strategy. The mindset accepts the presence of risk but focuses on calculated, reversible moves that create asymmetrical upside. For those with constrained income, the goal is not to gamble—it is to discover *micro-leverage*: where £10, £50, or £200 can make a disproportionate impact on earnings, skills, or autonomy.

There are three common objections that often prevent people from embracing this mindset: I don't have enough, I don't know how, and it's not for people like me. Each deserves scrutiny.

The first—*I don't have enough*—confuses quantity with viability. The idea that investment requires hundreds or thousands of pounds is largely outdated. Fractional investing platforms now allow access to markets with as little as £1. Skill-building platforms offer world-class education at marginal costs. Many side-income ventures require more effort than capital. While it is true that not all investments are accessible at every level, it is equally true that *some* are—and identifying those is the first exercise of an investment mindset.

The second—*I don't know how*—confuses complexity with danger. Finance can appear impenetrable, often by design.

But investing, at its root, is a behavioural art. You are not required to master derivatives or memorise ticker symbols to begin. What you do need is a framework for identifying opportunity and a discipline for prioritising it over short-term gratification. In most cases, the simplest forms of investment are also the most effective for beginners: broad-based index funds, short-term skill acquisition, and incremental ownership of productive tools.

The third—*it's not for people like me*—confuses narrative with truth. Media depictions of investors skew white, male, urban, and affluent. But investing has no demographic prerequisite. Every community has examples of resourceful, growth-minded individuals who made something from almost nothing. The challenge is not identity; it is access and narrative. Once someone internalises that investing is *a behaviour* and not *a status*, the path becomes less abstract. A mobile phone used to consume content becomes a tool for marketing freelance work. A public library becomes a learning centre. A community notice board becomes a source of clients. This is not romanticism. It is resourcefulness—a trait more common among low-income earners than finance textbooks acknowledge.

It is also worth addressing the cognitive friction involved in adopting this mindset. Many people working with limited financial means operate in survival mode. Under those conditions, the psychological space to think long-term shrinks. Research from behavioural economics shows that scarcity consumes cognitive bandwidth, reducing planning capacity and increasing the allure of immediate rewards. The investment mindset *pushes back* against this tendency. It creates a structure—however modest—where part of the mind is always scanning for multiplication, not just maintenance. Even the act of setting aside £5 per week for future opportunity signals to the brain that forward motion is possible.

From a policy and systems standpoint, this shift has implications too. When governments and financial institutions assume that investment begins at a certain income level, they exclude the very populations that would benefit most from early exposure to compounding tools. Inclusive finance isn't just about access to banking—it's about access to belief. To change outcomes, we must challenge the assumption that wealth-building begins *after* security. In reality, the two must be built together—often by the same pound.

In practical terms, a person living paycheque to paycheque may not be able to invest monthly in a stock index. But they *can* accumulate a growth fund over time. This might involve rounding up purchases, setting aside windfalls, or allocating a percentage of overtime earnings. They can also inventory their own skills, resources, and relationships for hidden assets—things that, with a small infusion of time or money, could yield disproportionate returns. Perhaps it's a language skill that can be monetised. A dormant business idea. A bike that, once repaired, opens access to delivery platforms. *The principle is to use money in ways that produce more of it*—directly or indirectly.

When this behaviour becomes habitual—when a person consistently looks for ways to convert income into opportunity—they build what might be called *financial reflexes*. Over time, these reflexes compound. The early investments may seem trivial, even invisible to others. But they lay the groundwork for a system that generates surplus, not just preserves it. And that surplus, once created, becomes the fuel for larger growth decisions—home ownership, business scaling, or early retirement.

None of this requires perfection. It requires orientation. Direction matters more than velocity. The investment mindset is not a destination you reach when you're rich enough, wise enough, or ready enough. It is a posture you adopt when you realise that *every pound is a choice*—not just a transaction. For those willing to make even small, strategic moves with clarity and consistency, the results can be transformative.

And so the question is not, *can you invest on a low income?* It is, *can you afford not to?* The compounding effects of time, attention, and strategic deployment are available to all—if you choose to think like an investor, rather than just a consumer. And in today's economy, that choice is not just financial. It is foundational.

Learning, Earning, and Ownership

The pursuit of financial growth is often portrayed as a linear path paved with spreadsheets, market charts, and compound interest calculators. But in practice, real-world wealth accumulation is built on three interdependent foundations: what you *know*, what you *earn*, and what you *own*. Each informs and reinforces the others. One's income ceiling is shaped by the skills they've acquired. Their asset base reflects not only past earnings, but how those earnings were allocated. And their ability to invest—strategically and consistently—is constrained or empowered by how much control they have over the underlying instruments of wealth creation. *To grow meaningfully, a person must learn, earn, and own—intentionally, iteratively, and in concert.*

Financial growth is typically framed as a question of investing—allocating money into instruments that multiply over time. But investing is only one species within a broader genus. If your portfolio grows but your income stagnates, your margin for contribution remains capped. If your earnings rise but you fail to acquire assets, you remain exposed to volatility. And if you own assets but lack the skills to manage or evolve them, they risk becoming liabilities. *Sustainable growth is integrative. It draws strength from multiple types of capital: financial, human, and productive.* Let us examine each in turn, not in isolation, but as part of a dynamic architecture for upward mobility.

Financial Capital: Making Money Make Money

This is the form of growth that receives the most attention—and often the least context. Investing in stocks, bonds, property, or businesses can be an extraordinarily effective engine of wealth, particularly when paired with time and consistency. But it must be approached not as a menu of options but as a set of responsibilities. The goal is not simply to acquire assets, but to understand them—how they behave under different economic conditions, how they generate returns, and how they align with one's broader life strategy.

A monthly investment into a broad-based index fund may yield average annual returns of 6–8% over time. But this only holds if the investor avoids panic-selling in downturns, maintains steady contributions through volatility, and understands the difference between risk and variance. *Knowledge is not ancillary to financial growth; it is a prerequisite.* Even modest investors—those allocating £50–£200 per month—can achieve significant results over time if their behaviour matches their intent. And those results, in turn, create optionality: funds for education, seed capital for ventures, or buffers against unforeseen events.

However, financial capital is not limited to passive investments. It includes productive capital—tools, platforms, or infrastructure that generate income. For a freelance graphic designer, a powerful laptop and design software are investments. For a part-time rideshare driver, a vehicle in good condition is not merely a cost—it is a lever.

The test is simple: *does this expenditure enable or accelerate the creation of future income?* If the answer is yes, it likely belongs in the Growth bucket.

Human Capital: Learning That Pays

Formal education is the most visible expression of skill-building, but it is rarely the most agile. In today's economy, adaptability often trumps accreditation. The ability to learn continuously, pivot quickly, and develop context-specific capabilities creates resilience and leverage in equal measure. Whether it's mastering a software platform, acquiring language fluency, learning negotiation tactics, or studying financial literacy, every skill has a potential yield—and the most valuable ones are often underpriced.

Human capital investments are powerful because their return is rarely linear. A £150 course in data visualisation may not yield immediate monetary benefit. But over time, it could enable a pay rise, unlock a freelance opportunity, or strengthen one's professional profile. Likewise, dedicating six months to evening language study may initially appear disconnected from income. But fluency might qualify the learner for international roles, client-facing positions, or translation gigs that would otherwise be inaccessible. *Growth in skills creates compounding value—not just in income, but in identity and optionality.*

Crucially, this kind of investment is available at every income level. A person earning minimum wage can still access free or low-cost educational platforms, community workshops, and public libraries. A single parent juggling shifts might not afford a £5,000 coding bootcamp, but they might afford 30 minutes of YouTube tutorials and a £20 textbook. The scale of investment matters less than the consistency. *Small, habitual skill-building changes trajectories in slow but irreversible ways.*

The risk, however, lies in confusion between learning and accumulation. Not all education is investment. Many pursue qualifications that lack clear application, relevance, or demand. The litmus test is pragmatic: *does this knowledge increase my ability to earn, build, or solve?* If not, it may be enrichment—but it is not growth. That distinction is essential in a world where attention and money are scarce resources.

Ownership: Building Stability and Agency

Ownership is often conflated with affluence: the house on the hill, the share portfolio, the rental flat. But at its core, ownership is about *control.* It is the difference between renting and shaping, between transacting and compounding. And in financial terms, it is the mechanism by which effort translates into enduring benefit.

When you own something that appreciates—or produces cash flow—you participate in its long-term upside. When you don't, your labour often enriches others while your own position remains static. This is clearest in housing: renters pay to access space, but homeowners build equity. Yet ownership is not universally superior. If a mortgage stretches one's finances too thin, it can reduce agility and increase vulnerability. The same applies to cars, businesses, or even digital assets. *Ownership is only empowering when it is sustainable.*

This is where the concept of assets versus liabilities becomes critical. Robert Kiyosaki popularised the distinction in *Rich Dad Poor Dad*, arguing that assets put money in your pocket, while liabilities take it out. The principle, though often oversimplified, remains useful. A car used for business can be an asset; a luxury car purchased on credit is likely a liability. A home that appreciates and supports lifestyle needs is an asset; one that induces chronic stress and eats discretionary income is not. *Ownership must be evaluated not by status, but by utility.*

For lower- and middle-income earners, paths to ownership can appear narrow. But they are not closed. Shared ownership schemes, micro-equity models, and cooperative enterprises are expanding. Digital assets—from eBooks to online courses—offer new ways to build intellectual property. Even small-scale business equipment, when owned outright, shifts power back to the individual. The goal is not to mimic the asset profiles of the wealthy, but to create *tailored vehicles of control* that generate cash flow, reduce dependency, and enable upward motion.

Critically, ownership is not just external. It includes one's reputation, brand, and relationships. A person who cultivates trust within a professional network owns something profoundly valuable—social capital. A creator with an audience owns leverage. A worker with repeat clients owns momentum. These intangible assets matter as much as the tangible, and they too require investment.

The Synergy of the Three

The most effective financial strategies are not siloed. They leverage the interplay between learning, earning, and ownership. A skill (learning) leads to higher income (earning), which funds a down payment (ownership), which appreciates and provides leverage for further investment (financial capital). This is not a theoretical model; it is how real people, over time, transform circumstances.

Take for example the story of James, a 28-year-old warehouse worker in Glasgow. With no university degree and a variable schedule, his prospects initially appeared modest. But he began using evenings to learn basic bookkeeping—first through free courses, then through a £99 online certificate. After six months, he began helping a cousin with invoicing for her hairdressing business. That side work led to referrals. A year later, he was managing books for six local small businesses, earning twice his warehouse pay. He registered as self-employed, bought his own laptop, and used surplus income to buy into a shared workspace co-op. Today, he owns a growing bookkeeping practice, employs a part-time assistant, and has saved enough to buy a small flat. *His arc is not the result of a windfall, but of layered investment—across knowledge, income, and control.*

For readers evaluating their own Growth bucket, the question is not which of the three categories is most urgent. It is *which lever can be moved today*. A £40 investment in learning. A £100 tool to launch a service. A shift from temporary gig work to stable part-time employment. Growth does not require brilliance or luck—it requires agency. When you spend to build capacity, you are no longer just consuming. You are constructing.

The traditional budget categories—food, rent, transport—are about survival. These three—learning, earning, ownership—are about *trajectory*. And the difference between the two is what ultimately defines whether money is just managed or *multiplied*. The Growth bucket is not a luxury reserved for the wealthy. It is the most practical, scalable tool for transforming limitation into leverage. The only requirement is to start.

How Much Is Enough?

The question of how much money to allocate toward growth is both urgent and deeply personal. Yet it is rarely answered with the clarity it deserves. Instead, people are offered vague slogans—"pay yourself first," "invest what you can," or "every little bit helps"—that may be emotionally reassuring but functionally useless. Others are handed aggressive formulas—"save 50%, invest 20%"—which ignore life stage, income variability, and context. The truth, as with most enduring financial insight, sits between abstraction and rigidity. *There is no universal rule. But there are intelligent benchmarks—anchored in purpose, calibrated by time horizon, and adjusted to human reality.*

To begin, it's worth reframing the question entirely. *"How much is enough?"* is not a question about quantity. It is a question about trajectory. The goal of growth allocation is not to hit an arbitrary target—it is to change the arc of one's financial capacity. A 22-year-old allocating 10% of their income toward growth may be building more effective long-term wealth than a 45-year-old investing 25% without clear intent. Similarly, a low-income household contributing £50 per month to a skill-building programme may be engaging in higher-yield growth spending than a high-income individual funnelling £500 into a mutual fund they don't understand.

This reframing matters because it removes guilt, bravado, and false comparison from the equation. *Enough* is not a number. It is the amount that meaningfully advances your financial potential, without destabilising the rest of your life. That threshold changes as you earn more, learn more, and gain more control over your obligations. What matters is not starting high, but starting *intentionally*—and then iterating upward.

Let's examine the key factors that shape this decision: income level, life stage, goal clarity, and surplus volatility. Together, they offer a framework—not a formula—for allocating toward growth with intelligence and sustainability.

Income Level and Allocation Elasticity

People earning below the median income often feel that growth is a luxury reserved for those with financial "breathing room." But this assumption confuses *amount* with *effectiveness*. A £25 monthly investment in a diversified fund, if maintained over decades, can grow into a five-figure sum. Likewise, a £15 monthly subscription to a skill-building platform can yield a pay rise that permanently alters one's earnings curve. Small amounts matter when they are consistent and leveraged.

The core principle here is elasticity. For someone earning £1,500 per month with fixed expenses of £1,200, the elasticity—the financial space within which discretionary decisions can be made—is £300. Asking this person to contribute 20% of their gross income (£300) to growth is unrealistic. But asking them to allocate 10–20% of their *surplus* (£30–£60) is achievable, if they understand what it can yield. In contrast, someone earning £4,000 per month with £2,500 in fixed costs has an elasticity of £1,500. For them, allocating 20–30% of gross income to growth may be not only feasible but essential—particularly if they aim to become work-optional within a defined timeframe.

The question is never just "how much do I earn?" It's "how much *flexibility* does my current lifestyle permit?" Growth allocation should come from that space—not from a sense of obligation, guilt, or mimicry.

Life Stage: Timing the Trade-offs

The optimal allocation toward growth also changes over time. In early adulthood, one's income is generally low, but time is abundant. This is the ideal moment to begin compounding—even in small doses—because the multiplier is not money, but time. The 24-year-old who begins investing £75 per month consistently is likely to outpace the 34-year-old who begins at £200, thanks to the exponential power of long-term returns. Similarly, learning investments made in one's twenties—such as gaining a second language, learning to code, or acquiring industry certifications—can have a multi-decade earnings impact.

In midlife, income typically rises, but so do obligations: mortgages, childcare, eldercare. This is when strategic prioritisation matters most. Rather than trying to maximise all categories simultaneously, individuals should ask: *what kind of growth will give me the most leverage in this season?* For some, that may be accelerating financial investments to catch up on retirement readiness. For others, it may mean diverting surplus income to home equity, or launching a side business that opens new revenue streams. What matters is that growth allocation does not default to the background just because other demands feel louder.

In later life, the definition of growth often shifts from accumulation to preservation and distribution. That does not make it less important. Continued investment in cognitive learning, community engagement, and legacy planning becomes a form of *intergenerational wealth strategy*.

Growth, here, is about expanding the impact of one's financial and human capital—not merely growing account balances.

Goal Clarity: What Is This Growth *For*?

Ambiguity is the enemy of consistency. People who do not know *why* they are allocating money toward growth will struggle to sustain it through volatility. Clear goals anchor action. These goals need not be rigid—"retire at 55 with £500,000"—but they should be coherent. Consider three distinct growth archetypes:

The *Stabiliser*: Someone seeking a safety net after years of financial precarity. For them, the Growth bucket may prioritise building a cash buffer, learning new income-generating skills, or eliminating high-interest debt.

The *Builder*: Someone with moderate stability aiming to expand upward. Their focus might be on investing regularly, acquiring assets, or increasing their earning power through education.

The *Scaler*: Someone with surplus income and foundational stability, now looking to optimise. They may invest in business ownership, advanced financial strategies, or high-impact philanthropy.

Each archetype carries different growth benchmarks. A Stabiliser may start with 5% of income toward growth. A Builder may target 15–20%. A Scaler might allocate 30–50%, especially if they are compressing time to financial independence. *The point is not to measure success by someone else's bar, but by alignment with your own season and strategy.*

Surplus Volatility and Dynamic Adjustment

Life rarely cooperates with fixed ratios. Bonuses arrive. Hours are cut. Kids get sick. Side hustles flourish, then falter. Growth allocations must respond accordingly. A static budget is a brittle budget. Instead, think in terms of *dynamic baselines*. For example: set a "minimum viable growth rate" (MVGR)—the smallest amount you will commit to growth even during tight months. For some, that might be £20. Then set a "stretch growth rate"—the percentage you will aim for during stable or surplus months. This might be 15% of surplus income or 10% of total income.

This system ensures continuity without rigidity. It also builds financial resilience. People who treat windfalls—tax returns, freelance payments, commissions—as opportunities to fund lifestyle upgrades often regress. But those who channel windfalls into high-leverage growth moves—debt repayment, seed capital, course tuition, lump-sum investing—create step-change improvements. *The gap between windfall and waste is usually determined by whether a growth plan already exists when the money arrives.*

Beyond Percentages: Growth as Design, Not Math

While benchmarks help guide allocation, they should never replace discernment. Two people could each invest 15% of income and end up with radically different outcomes, depending on what they invest in, how they manage behaviour, and whether their investments align with their evolving goals.

One person may spend 15% on a speculative crypto portfolio with no comprehension of risk. Another may spend the same amount on a series of professional development courses that double their income within three years. Both are allocating the same share of money—but only one is investing *with intelligence*. Similarly, some may choose to delay aggressive financial investing for five years while they fund a part-time degree or acquire a rental property. That delay, while appearing costly in isolation, may yield superior results over a lifetime.

This is why growth allocation is best viewed as *design*, not maths. It is a continual process of assessing trade-offs, timeframes, and temperament. The right allocation is not what looks good on paper—it's what advances your capacity while respecting your bandwidth. *Numbers matter, but strategy wins.*

A Final Calibration

For those seeking a practical starting point, here is a calibrated growth allocation framework:

If your fixed costs exceed 75% of income, and you're unable to save consistently: *start with 1–5% toward skill-building or debt reduction*. Your first win is not wealth, but *space*.

If your essentials fall between 50–70% of income: *allocate 10–20% toward a blend of learning and investing*, adjusting based on opportunity and urgency.

If your essentials are under 50%: *consider scaling to 30–40% growth allocation*, especially if you have clear medium-term goals such as financial independence, entrepreneurship, or early retirement.

These are not rules. They are *intelligent prompts*—starting points for design. Your life is not a spreadsheet, and your money map should reflect more than a formula. The question "how much is enough?" must be asked not once, but continually—as your income evolves, your aspirations expand, and your time horizon shifts.

Growth is not the product of perfect allocation. It is the cumulative outcome of thoughtful, sustained, flexible decisions—made with care, recalibrated often, and directed toward a future you have defined on your own terms.

From Surplus to Strategy

The most dangerous moment in personal finance is not when you're broke—it's when you finally have some breathing room. That first promotion, the unexpected bonus, the freelance project that pays off, the loan that's paid off—each creates a rare and fragile opportunity: the moment when "just enough" becomes "a little extra." What happens next defines the trajectory of financial independence or dependency. Most people, by default, choose lifestyle creep. But those who are prepared—those who have a surplus strategy—build the foundation for transformative growth.

The psychology of surplus is rarely discussed in financial education. We talk endlessly about scarcity: how to cut, budget, and survive. But we speak less often of what to do when we actually succeed in creating margin. This silence is costly. Without a conscious plan, new money becomes *invisible money*—absorbed seamlessly into elevated consumption. A pay rise becomes a car upgrade. A tax refund becomes a spontaneous holiday. What once felt like opportunity slowly becomes obligation. The upgraded becomes the expected, and the surplus vanishes.

To reverse this, we must shift our thinking: *surplus is not a reward—it is a resource*. It is not there to be congratulated, but deployed. It is not about feeling "deserving" of more, but *capable* of more. And like any high-value resource, surplus must be routed toward leverage—toward decisions that multiply our financial capability over time, rather than merely inflate our present comfort.

The first step is recognising surplus when it appears. This seems obvious, but in practice it is not. Many people do not register a pay rise or windfall as a surplus at all; they reframe it as a long-overdue correction. "Now I can finally afford..." becomes the unconscious script. To reclaim surplus as strategy, one must pre-decide: *any income or expense reduction that increases my financial margin is an opportunity—not just a relief*. This framing unlocks the potential of what economists call "marginal gains"—the small, often-overlooked improvements that compound meaningfully over time.

The second step is to *predefine the channels* into which surplus will be routed. Without a decision architecture, human behaviour defaults to emotional and social triggers. We spend because others do. We upgrade because it's "normal." We defer strategy because the reward of leisure, status, or convenience is more immediately gratifying than the abstract promise of compound growth. Predefined channels reverse this dynamic. They turn strategy into automation.

Consider a surplus-routing model composed of three core channels:

1. **Compounding Engines**—This includes investment accounts, retirement contributions, and business capital. These are mechanisms that turn money into more money without requiring constant input. They are essential because they scale disproportionately over time.

2. **Capability Builders**—These are expenditures that increase your future income-generating ability: education, certification, tools, or strategic relocation. Capability spending accelerates your earning curve, often more reliably than passive investment returns.

3. **Stability Buffers**—These include emergency funds, insurance coverage, and debt elimination. While less glamorous, they are what allow risk-taking in the other two

categories without financial fragility. They ensure that a temporary setback doesn't erase years of progress.

Routing surplus strategically means deciding—*before the money hits your account*—what portion will go to each category. For example: "Every surplus above my baseline budget gets split 50% to compounding, 30% to capability, 20% to buffer until targets are met." These ratios are not sacred; they are simply a starting point. The key is not perfection but intentionality. *If you don't assign your surplus, someone else—your past self, your peers, or the marketplace—will.*

Real-world application matters here. Consider the case of a mid-career professional who receives a £6,000 annual bonus. Without a routing plan, the bonus is typically absorbed into lifestyle: higher dining costs, shopping, a better car lease. Six months later, their savings remain unchanged. Contrast this with a routing strategy: £3,000 is invested into a diversified index fund, £2,000 funds a two-month data analytics course, and £1,000 goes to top up an emergency reserve. One year later, not only has the investment appreciated and the course led to a higher-paying role, but the emergency fund has avoided the use of credit during an unexpected dental bill. The same £6,000. A radically different outcome.

What makes this work is not the size of the surplus, but the clarity of the intention. Even modest surpluses can yield outsized returns. A part-time barista who reduces their rent by £100 per month by moving in with a friend has created

£1,200 per year in surplus. Routing half of that to a low-cost investing app and the other half to a personal development subscription can meaningfully improve their long-term trajectory. *Small, routed surpluses beat large, unstrategic windfalls every time.*

Some readers may object: "What if I just want to enjoy the money I've worked hard for?" The answer is not asceticism. It is proportionality. Strategic routing does not preclude enjoyment; it protects it. *There is no pleasure in lifestyle upgrades that increase stress, create new obligations, or crowd out future options.* The freedom to enjoy money comes not from spending all of it now, but from knowing you've secured the capacity to enjoy more later. A £300 surplus used to erase consumer debt offers far more enduring pleasure than the same amount spent impulsively on a weekend getaway that leaves no trace but a bill.

Philosophically, surplus routing is a practice in stewardship. It assumes that not all income is created equal. Baseline income pays for maintenance. Surplus income builds capacity. The tragedy of modern consumption is that we treat all income the same: available, expendable, and deserving of indulgence. But surplus is special. It carries the seed of *leverage*—the chance to earn more, keep more, and need less.

It's also worth acknowledging the *emotional discipline* surplus routing requires. We are not taught to think of money emotionally, but emotions drive behaviour. Without a conscious plan, we will respond to surplus the way our nervous system has been conditioned to respond: by reducing tension through reward. That's why impulse upgrades feel so natural. They signal safety, even if they erode it. Strategic surplus use, by contrast, often requires *delayed gratification, self-trust, and a future-oriented mindset.* These are muscles, not traits. They can be trained.

One powerful method is the *48-hour delay protocol*: whenever a new surplus appears—a freelance payment, a reduced expense, an unexpected refund—impose a two-day pause before making any new financial commitments. During that time, return to your routing framework. Ask: "What is the highest-leverage use of this money, given my goals and context?" Often, just this short reflection prevents low-utility consumption and redirects energy into growth-enhancing action.

Surplus routing also benefits from visibility. Create a dedicated "Opportunity Ledger"—a simple spreadsheet or notebook—where you log each surplus, its source, and how it was allocated. Over time, this becomes a record of momentum. A year's worth of small, strategic decisions documented in this way creates a sense of control and pride that no unplanned upgrade can match.

Finally, surplus strategy reinforces an essential truth of financial maturity: *wealth is not what you earn; it's what you keep and multiply.* Surplus is the space where that multiplication begins. But only if it's treated with respect. Without strategy, surplus becomes sand—disappearing between the fingers. With strategy, it becomes cement—the foundational material of upward mobility.

In every financial journey, there will be moments of margin—unexpected, irregular, and often temporary. The individuals who are prepared to use those margins wisely tend to build futures that seem disproportionate to their incomes. It is not magic. It is design. *And surplus, when routed strategically, is the most powerful design tool most people never use.*

Chapter 5
Safety—Designing a Resilient Life

Resilience is not the absence of upheaval; it is the ability to persist without faltering when disruption strikes. In the realm of personal finance, many presume that security is a natural by-product of wealth. Yet wealth—especially in the formative and mid-life stages—can be surprisingly delicate unless fortified by deliberate protective structures. The paradox is straightforward: one might be earning well, investing prudently, and managing expenses meticulously—and still be a single accident, diagnosis, or redundancy away from instability. Security is not a reward at the end of the journey; it is the scaffolding that makes the journey possible at all.

This chapter challenges a deeply ingrained assumption: that safety emerges purely from effort. Life, however, is probabilistic. Even the most meticulous plans succumb to entropy. True financial endurance does not arise from perfection; it arises from systems that can withstand stress and recover from shocks. This requires structures that operate effectively not only in ordinary circumstances but in extraordinary ones. Safety, therefore, is not a passive state—it is an intentional design choice.

Traditional financial guidance often reduces safety to a simple number: "Maintain three to six months of expenses in reserve." Yet this is a lazy prescription. Three to six months of what, precisely? Against whose volatility? For an individual with a secure government post, two months may be excessive. For a freelance parent with fluctuating income, six months might be perilously insufficient. The scale and shape of a safety net must be calibrated not to averages, but to exposure.

Instead of arbitrary targets, this chapter encourages viewing financial security as a system of buffers, tailored to one's risk profile across three domains: income, health, and liquidity. A young professional in good health, unencumbered by dependents and mobile in the job market, may prioritise flexible savings and short-term insurance. A single parent with a chronic health condition and irregular earnings must construct redundancy across income streams, housing stability, and critical coverage. Security is not a product—it is a configuration.

A more uncomfortable truth must also be confronted: most people fail to design safety systems because they mistake comfort for protection. Buying a high-end car with advanced airbags feels safer. Renting in a well-lit, expensive neighbourhood seems protective. Yet these upgrades often magnify financial fragility by raising baseline obligations. This is the psychology of false security: substituting the appearance of preparedness for its substance. A higher salary accompanied by longer commutes, strained mental health, or precarious job security is not protection—it is a liability masquerading as progress.

Insurance, too, requires re-examination—not as a checklist, but as an economic philosophy. Too often, insurance is regarded as something "one ought to have." In truth, it is the cost-effective outsourcing of catastrophic risk. Its value is not in averting minor inconvenience but in absorbing shocks that could otherwise erase years of accumulated progress. Yet households are frequently underinsured in areas that truly matter—disability, income protection—and overinsured in trivial domains, such as extended warranties for gadgets. The gap is rarely intention; it is framework: few know how to audit their risk landscape intelligently.

A useful concept from systems design is redundancy. In aviation, medicine, and military logistics, redundancy is not inefficiency—it is prudence. A commercial airliner has multiple engines not because dual failure is expected, but because failure is intolerable. Likewise, a robust financial system does not depend on a single income, savings account, or insurance policy. It builds strategic redundancy—not doubling every resource, but ensuring critical functions endure under stress.

Redundancy in personal finance translates into practical backups that avert panic. It means housing security even if a client payment is delayed. It means children retain access to essential medication despite job disruption. It means an unplanned dental procedure does not thrust one into high-interest debt. These scenarios are far from rare; they routinely unsettle otherwise stable households—not from negligence, but because their safety systems are cosmetic rather than structural.

The remedy is modularity, not maximalism. Resilience is less about overbuilding and more about constructing systems that can be repaired and rerouted. Consider a freelancer with three active clients, two months of readily accessible expenses, short-term income protection, and flexible rental arrangements. This individual is not "living in fear"; they are living strategically. Their lifestyle may appear modest, yet their financial engine is resilient. They neither scramble when a client vanishes nor spiral when their equipment fails—they operate with margin.

Margin is the true measure of safety. It is the space between obligations and resources, quantified not by status but by response capacity. How long could one maintain their standard of living if the primary income stopped? How many work hours could be reduced to care for a family member without destabilising bills? How often are choices made from opportunity rather than necessity? These are the real metrics of financial security, far surpassing income, property size, or job title.

Yet safety seldom dazzles. It rarely impresses on social media. The most financially resilient often appear unassuming by design. They maintain layers: emergency funds, liquidity lines, side income, cooperative housing, informal support networks. These invisible systems outweigh the sheen of polished appearances. Security is not displayed; it is felt—in the rarity of disruptions that can destabilise life.

This chapter revisits the emergency fund, repositioning it within a broader architecture of safety. Insurance is scrutinised for strategic utility rather than marketing allure. Lessons from engineering, logistics, and behavioural economics demonstrate that redundancy is a design principle, not inefficiency. Real-world application is central, exemplified through a case study of an independent creative who constructed a multi-layered financial shock absorber using the five-bucket model—tangible, actionable, and replicable.

The aim is not to instil anxiety, but to equip with the tools—intellectual and structural—to render risk non-fatal. Financial progress only matters if it is sustainable. Repeatability demands resilience. Growth expands, but safety preserves integrity. Without it, each step forward is hostage to fragility; with it, setbacks remain temporary. Ultimately, financial security is not the absence of threat—it is the presence of capacity to respond. And that capacity, with forethought and design, can be cultivated at any stage of life, regardless of income or circumstance.

Emergency Funds Reimagined – Most advice about emergency funds is arbitrary. This section reframes them as buffers that match your actual risk profile and volatility.

The prevailing advice about emergency funds has achieved the rare distinction of being widely accepted and profoundly misapplied. "Save three to six months' worth of living expenses" is repeated across personal finance literature, podcasts, and well-meaning dinner conversations with all the nuance of a refrigerator magnet slogan. Yet the moment one scrutinises this advice through the lens of behavioural risk, income volatility, or even basic opportunity cost, the cracks show. *Why three? Why six? Why not two, or nine, or an entirely different construct altogether?* The answer, more often than not, is inertia masquerading as prudence.

The core problem is that conventional emergency fund advice assumes homogeneity—that all lives, incomes, obligations, and risks can be addressed by the same prescriptive formula. This may make for tidy financial checklists, but it rarely holds up in practice. Consider the contrast between a salaried civil servant with tenure and subsidised healthcare, and a self-employed contractor whose income varies by project and whose entire livelihood depends on being physically well. To suggest both require the same financial buffer is to mistake equity for equality. *Safety is not measured in calendar months—it is measured in resilience to disruption.*

To rethink emergency funds properly, one must first discard the idea that there is a universally "right" number. Instead, *start with the volatility you actually face*. This includes income volatility (how predictable is your cash flow?), expenditure rigidity (how many of your monthly costs are truly fixed?), and fragility exposure (what is the probability of a sudden, significant expense?). A person with stable but low income and high prescription costs may need a different buffer strategy than someone with lumpy freelance earnings but minimal fixed outgoings. A retiree with no earned income but significant invested assets is in yet another category altogether. *Financial safety is contextual, not categorical.*

There is also the overlooked matter of access. Many people technically *have* assets, but lack liquidity. They are "asset-rich, cash-poor"—a home with equity but no buffer for a dental emergency. Or they've amassed retirement savings but would face penalties or tax liabilities for early withdrawal. A properly designed emergency fund, therefore, must meet two thresholds: *relevance* (it covers the type of risk you are exposed to) and *readiness* (it can be accessed without incurring additional damage). A £10,000 buffer that takes 14 days to liquidate and imposes a 10% penalty is not an emergency fund. It is a mirage.

Equally problematic is the assumption that all emergencies are catastrophic in size. In practice, most financial shocks are incremental, not apocalyptic. A delayed client payment. A cracked phone screen. An unexpected prescription. What these events share is not magnitude, but *timing misalignment*. They arrive before your next paycheque, or during a period of heightened obligation, or just as a different financial plan was in motion. For most households, it is not the *size* of an emergency that breaks the system—it is the *lack of absorption capacity*. Thus, an emergency fund isn't just about survival—it's about maintaining *trajectory*. A buffer exists so progress is not undone by interruption.

The new model for thinking about emergency funds is as follows: *You are not protecting against bad luck. You are designing for bad timing.* With this framing, the questions change. Instead of asking "how much do I need?", we ask:

How long could I go without income before compromising my obligations?

What are the most probable types of disruptions I face (medical, employment, housing)?

What other support systems exist that I can reliably access (insurance, family, community, credit)?

How can I layer my buffers so that smaller shocks don't consume the entire safety net?

Answering these with rigour leads to a multi-tiered model of emergency preparedness. The first tier is *rapid-access liquidity*—an amount that covers immediate shortfalls (typically one to two weeks of core spending). This is the cash in your account that means a car repair doesn't derail your rent payment. The second tier is *intermediate resilience*—resources you can tap within a few days without penalty (high-yield savings, flexible investments, low-cost credit with pre-approval). The final tier is *structural resilience*—your ability to adjust lifestyle, negotiate with creditors, activate insurance, or draw upon community or institutional support in sustained hardship. *An emergency fund is not a single sum—it is an ecosystem of response options.*

Consider also the psychological architecture of emergency buffers. An overly large emergency fund sitting idle in cash can produce a sense of stagnation—especially in low-interest environments where inflation erodes its value. The individual begins to question whether they are being cautious or simply inefficient. This is not a trivial concern. Financial systems that are psychologically alienating tend not to last. Therefore, where possible, emergency buffers should be designed to feel *purposeful,* not punitive. Segregated accounts, labelled goals, or using sweep automation can help preserve the buffer without triggering a scarcity mindset. *A healthy buffer is one that protects you not just financially, but cognitively—it allows you to think clearly under pressure.*

The goal, ultimately, is to align your buffer with your *risk contour*. If you are young, healthy, low-debt, and high-agility, your emergency fund can afford to be lean and nimble. If you are older, dependent-heavy, or in an economically unstable sector, you will want deeper and more layered defences. None of this requires panic. What it requires is precision. The average emergency fund guidance is a product of convenience, not comprehension. The new model asks more of you—but in return, it offers a buffer that *actually works when it is most needed.*

For example, in a recent study of gig economy workers in the UK, those who segmented their financial buffers into specific tiers reported higher confidence in facing irregular income months, despite earning less annually than salaried peers. Their buffers were not necessarily larger, but they were *better matched to the shape of their volatility*. This is a crucial distinction. You don't need more money—you need *the right configuration of readiness*.

Furthermore, by defining "emergency" more narrowly—situations where the absence of cash would *compound harm*—we become more surgical in how we allocate funds. Not every inconvenience deserves a withdrawal from the buffer. A flat tyre is an annoyance, not a crisis. But if it means missing work and losing income for the week, it *becomes* a crisis. Context determines classification. Which means buffer design must also be dynamic. *A static emergency fund for a dynamic life is, by definition, a mismatch.*

Finally, it is time to update the language. Rather than "emergency fund," which implies passivity and binary use, we might adopt the term *resilience reserve*. This is money whose purpose is not just protection, but *continuity*. It is the capital that allows you to pivot instead of panic. To absorb shocks without compromising future leverage. To buy time, not just solve problems. In this way, emergency funds are not about fear. They are about *freedom*. The freedom to keep moving when things go wrong. The freedom to make decisions from strategy, not desperation. The freedom to weather risk *on your own terms*.

In reimagining emergency funds, we're not discarding traditional wisdom—we're refining it. We are applying intelligence to intuition. Specificity to generality. And, crucially, *adaptation to standardisation*. Because the future is not static, and your buffer shouldn't be either. If financial growth is about moving forward, financial safety is about *being able to keep going*. And that—when designed with insight—is worth far more than six months of expenses sitting silently in an unnamed account.

Insurance, Not Illusion – We dig into the psychology of false security, and what true protection looks like—from health coverage to job redundancy planning

The greatest misunderstanding in personal finance is not about money—it is about safety. People often believe they are protected when they are merely pacified. They purchase insurance policies, draft emergency plans, or open savings accounts with the quiet confidence that risk has been neutralised. But *risk is not neutralised by paperwork; it is neutralised by design*. And the modern consumer, seduced by language and lulled by glossy assurances, frequently mistakes *coverage* for *comprehensiveness*, and *premiums* for *peace of mind*.

True financial protection is not a product—it is an architecture. And understanding this distinction is essential to building resilience that works when it matters most. Insurance, as commonly understood, is sold as an antidote to anxiety. But psychologically, it often functions more like a sedative. *People sleep better knowing they have it, but few understand what it actually does*. The gap between perceived protection and actual coverage is not just a detail—it is the risk itself.

Health insurance offers one of the clearest examples of this illusion. Many individuals believe that simply possessing a policy means they are "covered," yet remain unaware of exclusions, co-payments, limits, or out-of-network penalties. In the United Kingdom's NHS system, this disconnect shows up differently: while citizens may not worry about treatment access, they often conflate universal coverage with universal sufficiency. A policy may *entitle* one to care, but not *guarantee* timeliness, choice, or outcome. Thus, a diagnosis requiring rapid intervention can reveal a sobering truth—*legal access is not logistical readiness*. And no amount of printed entitlements can fill the gap between what is theoretically available and what is pragmatically deliverable.

Similar distortions occur with income protection and redundancy insurance. In theory, they are designed to soften the blow of job loss or long-term illness. In practice, they are often riddled with waiting periods, strict definitions of "inability to work," or vague terms that favour the underwriter over the claimant. The customer believes they are covered "if something happens." But few interrogate *what exactly must happen, how soon after, to what extent,* and *for how long*. When the moment of crisis arrives, they discover that what they own is not a safety net, but a spiderweb—visible, but unable to support any meaningful weight.

The deeper issue, however, is not the structure of insurance contracts but the psychology that surrounds them. We crave certainty in uncertain systems. And when complexity overwhelms comprehension, we default to signals of safety. This is why the mere *act of insuring* feels responsible—even when the coverage is inadequate. It is also why many forgo critical policies altogether. The mental model is binary: either you are insured, or you're not. But this is a false dichotomy. *The real question is not whether you are covered, but whether you are protected.*

True protection is a strategy, not a signature. It requires knowing your dependencies—income, health, housing, continuity—and mapping them against both likelihood and impact. What would derail your life most immediately?

What would compromise your future most enduringly? Protection that aligns with these realities is often unglamorous and less advertised. It is the boring stuff—term life insurance, critical illness cover, durable power of attorney, diversified income plans—that provides real ballast. And because these do not advertise their virtues through everyday transactions, they are often neglected until they are urgently needed.

Part of the solution is linguistic. The term "insurance" itself misleads. It implies a bet against misfortune—a wager that you hope to lose. But in practice, the best forms of protection are not about betting—they're about *buffering*. When designed properly, a protection plan isn't hoping to cover losses; it is ensuring *continuity of function*. The emphasis shifts from reimbursement to resilience. The test of a good plan is not how much money it returns in crisis, but how little your life must change in its aftermath.

Another part of the solution is structural. Instead of seeing insurance as the answer, we must see it as *one layer* in a wider safety system. Think of this in tiers. At the base lies self-insurance: your capacity to absorb small shocks through savings, flexibility, and redundancy. Next is formal insurance: well-designed policies tailored to your actual exposures, not generic templates. Above that are informal networks—family, community, employers, and state systems. Finally, at the top is *strategic optionality*: the capacity to pivot, retrain, relocate, or reinvent when a path closes. *Real security lies not in predicting every risk, but in remaining agile when the unpredictable strikes.*

To illustrate, consider two households with identical incomes and living costs. Household A allocates a portion of their budget to premium comprehensive insurance policies—private health, full vehicle cover, extensive gadget insurance—believing this "buys peace of mind." Household B takes a different approach. They carry only essential insurance—health and liability—but maintain a six-month liquidity reserve, cross-train in multiple income streams, and own their home outright. On paper, Household A appears more protected. In reality, Household B has layered protection: if one layer fails, another absorbs the strain. Household A, dependent on claim approval and policy interpretation, is more exposed than they realise.

The problem isn't just technical—it's cultural. Insurance companies often market security as a finished product. Buy this, and you're safe. But *safety is not a one-time purchase; it is an ongoing configuration.* It requires vigilance, not just compliance. Policies must be reviewed annually. Life circumstances shift—marriage, children, health changes, asset accumulation—and with them, the types of risk you must account for. Failing to update your protection architecture is like using last year's weather forecast to plan today's wardrobe. Eventually, you will be caught unprepared.

Equally important is clarity of objective. Insurance is not there to make you whole—it is there to *keep you afloat*. Many policies sell the illusion of restoration: that you'll be compensated enough to return to your previous state. But this is rarely the case. Time, stress, disruption, and bureaucracy all take their toll. A payout might offset bills, but it cannot erase interruption. Thus, the better strategy is *minimisation of disruption, not compensation for disaster*. That means building your own buffers alongside any policy—cash flow redundancy, time flexibility, digital backups, and knowledge assets.

Psychologically, people also confuse *affordability* with *effectiveness*. The monthly premium is visible; the contract's exclusions are not. And many fall into a trap of "coverage shopping"—buying too many policies with overlapping features while still leaving core vulnerabilities unaddressed. A well-structured protection plan begins not with "what can I afford to insure?" but with "what can I *not* afford to lose?" The hierarchy of needs must shape the hierarchy of cover. Start with income replacement. Then health. Then liability. Then property. Then lifestyle. Not all risks are created equal, and financial resilience depends on being able to distinguish between a nuisance and a collapse.

Ultimately, true protection is not about paranoia—it is about preparedness. It does not require you to fear the worst, but to *be ready for disruption*. The most resilient individuals are not those with the most coverage, but those with the most *clarity*. They know where they are exposed. They know which tools mitigate which threats. And they review their safeguards not as a box-ticking exercise, but as a continuous part of financial stewardship.

The illusion of insurance is that it replaces personal responsibility. The truth of insurance, when used properly, is that it *enables* personal responsibility. It buys time to think, space to act, and options when clarity is most scarce. But it is only one piece of the architecture. Real security comes from how that piece fits into the whole.

To build resilience is not to eliminate risk—it is to *design around it*. And that requires not just paperwork, but *presence of mind*. When protection is approached with that clarity, insurance stops being an illusion and becomes what it was meant to be: a tool. Not a promise, not a placebo, but a precise part of a larger system—one that keeps you moving, adapting, and secure on *your* terms.

Redundancy and Optionality – Drawing from systems design and military logistics, we explain why having backup plans is a form of wealth

Most people misunderstand redundancy. They see it as waste—an extra tool, an unused subscription, an idle plan. In the language of efficiency, redundancy appears undesirable. It violates the aesthetic of minimalism and the cultural myth of lean optimisation. But in any system where failure has real consequences, *redundancy is not wasteful—it is wise*. And when applied to personal finance, career strategy, or life planning, it becomes not just wise but *wealth-generating*.

In systems design, redundancy is not a luxury—it is a requirement for resilience. Whether engineering spacecraft or managing a supply chain, mission-critical systems are built to withstand shock. This means not relying on a single power source, communication line, or operational path. If Plan A fails, Plan B is not improvised—it's built in. NASA doesn't consider an Apollo mission safe unless it can complete its objective even if multiple systems fail. Commercial aircraft operate with triple-redundant flight control systems—not because they expect failure, but because they *refuse to be at the mercy of it*.

The same mindset applies in military logistics. Redundancy is the reason militaries stockpile equipment, over-provision fuel, and maintain satellite alternatives to ground communications. When the environment becomes unstable—whether geopolitical, economic, or technological—survival and success depend on *options*. The presence of backup isn't inefficiency—it's power.

In personal finance, however, this mindset is often absent. People optimise their budgets, schedules, and careers down to the wire. They automate transfers to a single investment account. They rely on one employer, one bank, one internet provider, one income stream. On paper, it looks lean. But the system is brittle. *And brittle systems fail quietly until they fail catastrophically.*

Wealth, properly understood, is not just stored value—it's strategic slack. It is the ability to absorb disruption without panic, to reroute rather than retreat. Redundancy makes this possible. The freelancer with two steady clients and a pipeline of three more is wealthier—in resilience terms—than the salaried professional with no fallback and a 60-hour work week. The tenant with savings, family support, and remote work eligibility is more secure than the homeowner leveraged to the hilt and bound to a single city. *The real measure of wealth is not how well your life works when everything goes right—it's how little it collapses when things go wrong.*

Optionality is the companion principle to redundancy. Where redundancy is the duplication of capability, optionality is the expansion of choice. The systems that endure volatility are not those with the highest capacity, but those with the most *degrees of freedom*. This is why evolutionary biology favours species with adaptable diets, why financial markets reward instruments with liquidity, and why personal resilience depends on *having more than one way forward*.

A person with three skillsets is not just more employable—they are more powerful. A household with low fixed costs is not just thriftier—they are more manoeuvrable. Optionality transforms surplus into strength. It lets you say no to bad deals, walk away from toxic environments, and take intelligent risks without being recklessly exposed. It grants time, perspective, and leverage. And in the 21st century, *leverage is one of the few forms of power available to individuals at scale.*

This is not about hoarding. It is not about prepping for apocalypse or stacking backups until life becomes unlivable. It is about intentional design—building a life where failure is tolerated, not fatal. This includes redundancy in income: cultivating side projects, developing monetisable skills, diversifying professional relationships. It includes redundancy in expenses: maintaining buffer capacity in your budget, avoiding overspecialisation in lifestyle, staying adaptable in housing and transport. And it includes redundancy in decision-making: maintaining multiple mental models, keeping opposing truths in view, never betting the entire outcome on a single assumption.

Consider an individual working in a volatile industry—let's say media or tech. The job pays well, but layoffs are common and career paths are nonlinear. The employee with redundancy has emergency savings, freelance experience, and an adjacent qualification (perhaps in marketing, analytics, or policy). If the company collapses, their options don't. They can shift sideways, downshift strategically, or take a sabbatical without existential panic. They do not *need* a miracle—they just need a plan. And they've already built three.

Contrast this with someone who has built a life where every system depends on everything working perfectly. The income barely covers the mortgage. The job requires commuting to a single city. The children attend a school that can't be easily changed. The skills are niche. The debt is structured around optimistic projections. This is not a lack of wealth—it's a lack of *option*. And when constraints tighten, people without options are forced into expensive decisions.

Redundancy, then, is not inefficient—it is cost-saving over time. It lowers the price of failure and raises the ceiling on risk. The person with optionality can say yes to the opportunity others must reject. They can start the business, move to the new city, or leave a bad employer. Not because they're brave, but because they are *positioned*. Their system has been designed not just for optimisation—but for *adaptation*.

The corporate world understands this. Smart companies never operate with a single supplier, a single data centre, or a single leadership strategy. Redundant systems are budgeted as essential infrastructure. So why do individuals settle for single points of failure? Why is it considered extravagant to hold a second skillset, a second income stream, or a second living option?

The answer is psychological. Redundancy feels unnecessary until the moment it becomes critical. People avoid the discomfort of planning for failure because they conflate optimism with clarity. But *clarity is not about predicting disaster—it's about preparing for possibility*. To treat redundancy as pessimism is to misunderstand its function. It is not a bet against yourself—it is a vote for your continuity. It says: no matter what changes, I will still have room to move.

This applies to identity as well. People often over-identify with a single role—breadwinner, homeowner, expert, provider—and anchor their financial systems to that role. But life is fluid. Identity shifts. Roles evolve. And when you are only one thing, your fall is total. Redundancy in identity—being a learner, a contributor, a generalist, an adapter—provides not just financial elasticity, but *psychological durability*. It lets you reinvent without shame, pivot without crisis, and grow without fear of irrelevance.

In design terms, redundancy is a function of *intentional inefficiency*. It's about building for the unknown by accepting that over-optimised systems are not resilient systems. You do not need to spend twice. You need to spend *flexibly*. A tool that does one thing brilliantly is less valuable in a crisis than a tool that does three things adequately. Your financial life should operate the same way.

Optionality and redundancy are not distractions from your goals—they are *enablers* of them. They make your ambitions less fragile, your timelines less rigid, and your energy more sustainable. And in a world where volatility is rising—economic, technological, ecological—these traits are no longer luxuries. They are prerequisites for sovereignty.

Ultimately, redundancy and optionality are wealth in their most elegant form: *not just what you own, but what you can afford to lose*. Not just how much you earn, but how little you *must* earn to remain free. Not just how fast you grow, but how slowly you can afford to retreat when necessary.

Design your systems accordingly. Optimise not just for performance, but for survival. Build not just for today's goals, but for tomorrow's unknowns. Redundancy is wealth. Optionality is power. *And the freedom to manoeuvre is a form of security that no salary alone can buy.*

Case Study: The Freelancer's Financial Shock Absorber – A narrative of how one independent worker created a multi-layered safety net using the 5-bucket lens

At first glance, Ava's financial life appeared precarious. She was a self-employed graphic designer in her mid-thirties with no employer pension, no paid sick leave, and no guaranteed income. Her client roster changed every quarter, her earnings fluctuated with the market, and there were no colleagues to split the load if she got ill or took time off. From a traditional financial planning lens, she looked like a high-risk case. Yet during the pandemic, a prolonged illness, and two years of inflationary headwinds, Ava didn't just survive—she moved into a more stable flat, funded a sabbatical, and quietly doubled her net worth. Her secret wasn't a windfall. It was *structure.*

What made Ava's financial system resilient wasn't high income or perfect forecasting—it was an intentional use of the five-bucket budget framework to build in *layers of self-insurance*. Each bucket acted not just as a spending category but as a dynamic stabiliser, calibrated to the volatility of freelance life. The system didn't prevent shocks, but it absorbed them—quietly, efficiently, and without emotional drama.

Ava's baseline income fluctuated between £3,500 and £6,000 per month. That variability would be anxiety-inducing for many, but Ava saw it as an architectural challenge, not a personal failing. She began by decoupling *earnings* from *lifestyle*. Her Essentials bucket—rent, utilities, groceries, insurance—was tightly calibrated to her lowest three-month average income. She chose a modest flat in a walkable neighbourhood, gave up her car in favour of cycling and car-sharing, and set up a shared co-working membership rather than a full-time private studio. The aim wasn't austerity—it was *predictability*. By lowering her fixed cost floor, she gained breathing room at the top.

Her discretionary Lifestyle bucket—restaurants, holidays, hobbies—operated with strict modularity. She funded it using a separate debit card loaded monthly from a sub-account. When income was lean, this allocation shrank seamlessly. When she had a surge month, she didn't automatically expand her spending. Instead, she rerouted the overflow into her *Growth bucket*—but not in the typical, narrow sense of retirement investing.

For Ava, growth spending was tri-dimensional: she split it between financial investments, skills development, and long-term ownership plays. When work was plentiful, she funded her ISA and brokerage account. When client leads slowed, she shifted focus to certifications in UX design and data visualisation—leveraging free time into higher future rates. This adaptive allocation was *not* reactive. It was governed by a pre-set decision tree she updated each January, allowing her to act quickly without second-guessing.

The real genius of Ava's system, however, lay in how she treated the Safety bucket. While most freelancers aim for a three- or six-month emergency fund, Ava took a more nuanced approach. She didn't define safety by duration, but by *function*. Her safety net had four distinct layers:

1. **Fast-access liquidity:** A high-yield instant-access savings account holding the equivalent of one month's baseline expenses. This wasn't just for true emergencies—it covered late payments, short dry spells, or unexpected dental work.

2. **Income smoothing buffer:** A rolling surplus account into which she deposited any income above her monthly essentials plus lifestyle cap. This gave her the ability to draw a fixed "salary" even when client payments lagged. It also acted as an early warning system—when the buffer dropped below £1,500, she shifted into acquisition mode and activated her "client pipeline sprint" routine.

3. **Contingency reserves:** A separate savings vault, labelled "Stability Reserve," equal to roughly four months of baseline expenses. This was for true structural disruptions—health issues, market slowdowns, or major transitions like moving house or taking family leave. She

tapped it only twice in five years, but its existence meant she never had to borrow under pressure.

4. **Time capital:** Perhaps most importantly, Ava saved up what she called "freedom fuel"—enough money to take a three-month sabbatical every three to four years. During one such break, she retooled her portfolio, exited two emotionally draining retainer clients, and created a course that became a passive income stream. Without that pause, she later reflected, her burnout would have sabotaged her long-term income far more than any market fluctuation.

Ava's Giving bucket was modest in financial terms but consistent in execution. She donated 2% of her income each quarter to causes she pre-vetted in January and volunteered her design services twice a year to small non-profits. These acts weren't peripheral—they were part of her psychological stabiliser. Giving reminded her that money was not just a survival tool but a lever for contribution. In volatile months, that mental framing helped her stay anchored.

What's striking is how *mechanical* Ava's system had become—not in a robotic sense, but in terms of *removing emotional reactivity*. Her budgetary habits weren't driven by guilt, ambition, or scarcity panic. They were pre-decided, reviewed quarterly, and tuned to her actual volatility curve. That curve, in turn, was informed by her freelance history—she knew the seasonal patterns, the length of her average dry spell, the payment lags of her anchor clients. She didn't *hope* things would be stable—she *built* stability into the system.

This approach stands in contrast to many personal finance narratives that focus on discipline or self-denial. Ava's model is not built on restraint but *resilience*. She doesn't try to forecast everything or control every outcome. Instead, she designs for uncertainty. And crucially, she doesn't just accumulate money—she accumulates *capacity*. Time capacity, decision capacity, mental bandwidth, skill versatility. Her net worth is a by-product, not the sole measure, of financial health.

Ava's story also offers an implicit critique of advice that treats budgeting as static. A 50/30/20 rule or a fixed savings rate might serve salaried workers with stable incomes—but for freelancers, that rigidity can become self-defeating. What they need is a system with *shock absorbers*, not just dashboards. The five-bucket framework gave Ava that flexibility: each bucket had both a structural role and a dynamic function. They absorbed not just expense categories but *changes in volatility, seasonality, and energy*.

Some of Ava's choices might not appeal to everyone. Not every freelancer can downsize housing, or go without a car, or design digital products. But the broader point transcends specific tactics. Ava didn't just diversify her income—she diversified her *stability inputs*. She didn't treat her business income as sacred and the rest of her life as reactive. Instead, she created feedback loops: when work was high, growth accelerated; when work was low, skill-building or rest took priority. There was no binary between thriving and surviving—only continuous rebalancing.

Perhaps the most powerful insight from Ava's system is this: *true security for freelancers doesn't come from maximising revenue—it comes from mastering the shape of risk.* Ava couldn't prevent income dips, but she ensured that no single month could spiral into a crisis. She didn't need a crystal ball—she needed a circuit-breaker. And that's what the 5-bucket method delivered.

Financial independence isn't always about leaving work behind—it's about *choosing your work from a place of clarity, not desperation.* Ava still works hard. But she does it with agency. Her system gives her something most freelancers lack: a quiet confidence that even when things shift, *nothing essential will break.* Her buckets hold not just cash—but composure. And in a world where volatility is the norm, *composure is its own form of capital.*

Chapter 6
Joy—Permission to Spend

Modern budgeting frameworks often carry an implicit assumption: that life's pleasures are best postponed indefinitely, awaiting some abstract financial horizon. Happiness becomes conditional, granted only once retirement accounts are maxed, debts cleared, emergency funds stocked, and property secured. Yet the absence of joy is far from costless—it accrues quietly, compounding in ways that discipline alone cannot counter. When our lives offer no deliberate space for pleasure, beauty, or meaning, the psyche tends to seek compensation in spending that masquerades as leisure: impulsive purchases, binge travel, or other numbing habits. Prudence slips away; what remains is a poverty of intention. The Joy bucket exists precisely to contest that drift.

Allocating for joy is not a lapse in discipline—it is its most sophisticated expression. Human beings are not spreadsheets. We are not optimisation machines. We are finite creatures with emotional thermometers, and when these reserves are depleted, decision-making suffers—financially, relationally, and physically. Neglecting joy is not frugality; it is attrition. Over time, it erodes the psychological musculature upon which every other financial bucket depends.

And yet, despite this reality, joy is the bucket most frequently underfunded. Not because resources are lacking, but because permission is absent. High achievers, in particular, often view joy spending as indulgence to be earned rather than a function to be respected. These are the very individuals who, dutifully maxing out pensions and sacrificing small pleasures, risk burnout while maintaining the illusion of relentless forward motion. Intelligence is not the problem; framing is. Treat joy as peripheral, and it leaks; systematise it, and it becomes leverage.

This chapter is not an exhortation to self-indulgence. It is a call to design. What is joy worth to you—not in abstraction, but in your monthly budget? Money is not an end in itself; it is a means to fund a life that feels complete. And completeness requires moments that resist purely productive or justifiable framing.

Financial institutions largely ignore joy because it defies optimisation. Essentials can be calculated, growth modelled, safety quantified—but joy resists metrics. Its value is subjective. One person finds it in a monthly ceramics class, another in a weekend with friends, or the quiet dignity of a well-hosted dinner. No universal formula exists, which is why the approach must be personal.

Yet personal need not mean arbitrary. Joy spending demands intentionality—perhaps more than any other category—because its function is as emotional as it is economic. Left unattended, it morphs into two unhelpful extremes: joyless consumption—endless streaming subscriptions barely used—or compensatory splurges—a sudden £3,000 getaway after months of burnout. Neither generates lasting satisfaction. The solution is not abstinence, but thoughtful design.

Designing for joy begins with definition. Many struggle because they never pause to identify what genuinely brings happiness—not stimulation, not status, but joy itself.

Reflection of this sort may feel indulgent, especially for those steeped in cultures of utility and sacrifice. Yet it is foundational, allowing us to cease funding phantom pleasures and redirect resources toward experiences that truly matter.

This chapter will provide prompts to surface those insights and structure their application. The Joy bucket is not simply about spending money on pleasant things; it is about engineering emotional resonance. Behavioural science proves useful here. Research shows that modest, well-planned experiences yield more enduring happiness than impulsive, costly purchases. The secret lies in anticipation and memory—two invisible multipliers of satisfaction.

A £40 concert ticket bought weeks in advance creates an arc: the pleasure of anticipation, the experience itself, and the afterglow of memory. Compare this to a £400 designer item acquired on impulse: a narrow spike of satisfaction that decays rapidly, often with buyer's remorse as garnish. Joy is not a price tag; it is emotional return. And that return grows with intention and diminishes with reactivity.

Understanding this dismantles the myth that joy is reserved for the wealthy. Some of the richest experiences occur on modest incomes precisely because they are deliberate. A grandmother who budgets £25 to take her granddaughter out for breakfast, a student who forgoes takeaways to afford a train ticket to see their partner—these are not indulgences, but investments in meaning.

Crucially, joy is not always transactional. Nor does "free" automatically qualify as joy. The aim of this bucket is not to monetise happiness but to safeguard its space. Money is a tool, not a prerequisite. For some, it funds solitude—a quiet Airbnb to reflect or write. For others, shared experiences: gatherings, rituals, holidays. Conscious decision-making is key. Unexamined spending, even on things we enjoy, rarely registers as genuine joy.

This distinction matters especially in low-income households, where joy spending can feel morally questionable. Even small indulgences may trigger guilt. Yet without joy, the will to persist erodes. Families who embed modest celebrations—Friday takeaways, birthday outings, small treats—are not being reckless; they are protecting morale. And morale is a financial asset, fueling perseverance, cohesion, and forward motion.

Joy spending is also distinct from lifestyle creep. The latter is reactive, expanding in lockstep with income, often unconsciously. The Joy bucket is proactive, tethered to values rather than earnings. Someone on £25,000 can curate a more coherent Joy bucket than a £250,000 earner who spends without awareness. The objective is not to mirror others' pleasures but to fund your own.

Interestingly, joy underpins financial sustainability. Budgets that include joy are easier to adhere to, because deprivation is mitigated. A budget that reflects values, rather than punishment, allows scarcity to lose its grip. Discipline becomes curation, not constraint.

Yet ambition often encourages deferral: joy will come later, after the next milestone, once the mortgage is paid, once the business turns a profit. Deferred joy, however, is frequently neglected joy. Life's texture is woven in weeks and weekends, dinners and walks, spontaneous detours and planned delights. If money is not supporting any of that now, it is worth asking why.

This chapter does not champion hedonism or distraction. It advocates integration: placing joy not at the periphery of financial life, but within its architecture. Joy is not optional—it is a signal of vitality. And when funded with intention, it elevates more than spending; it elevates living itself.

The Bucket Everyone Neglects

There is a quiet irony in modern personal finance: the very people who are most competent at managing money often deny themselves the one category designed to preserve their humanity. Among high-performers—doctors, entrepreneurs, analysts, educators, artists—there is a consistent and conspicuous omission in how budgets are allocated: they account meticulously for obligations, prudently for growth, cautiously for safety, yet almost apologetically for joy. The underlying belief is rarely articulated but deeply embedded—joy is indulgence, something earned only after duty is fulfilled, never budgeted for as part of it. The consequence of this mindset is not only emotional depletion but financial misalignment. When joy is ignored, it doesn't disappear. It mutates. And the result is not greater discipline, but greater vulnerability to burnout, resentment, and reactive spending. *Neglecting joy is not a sign of maturity—it is a strategic oversight.*

High-achievers tend to confuse deferred gratification with moral virtue. They take pride in delaying pleasure, in prioritising outcomes over experiences. On the surface, this looks like stoicism. In reality, it often masks chronic self-disregard. What begins as focus can harden into asceticism—until the system breaks. And when it does, correction doesn't arrive in the form of a quiet course adjustment; it comes as collapse. Relationships fray. Health declines. Impulsive purchases surge. Travel is booked in desperation, not celebration. A sabbatical is taken not for vision but recovery. These are not luxuries gone awry—they are symptoms of a budget that failed to account for the whole person.

The Joy bucket, as proposed in the Five-Bucket framework, is not a decorative extra. It is a structural necessity. It anticipates what most financial systems ignore: that people are not just earners or savers—they are emotional beings with thresholds. The consistent neglect of this category by high-achievers is not a personal flaw, but a predictable byproduct of how success is culturally coded. Reward is external. Productivity is sacred. And pleasure, unless it signals status, is suspect. In this model, joy must be justified. It must be "deserved," often in proportion to exhaustion.

But joy cannot function as compensation for burnout. *It is preventive maintenance, not emergency response.* Just as regular exercise prevents illness and proactive sleep staves off fatigue, regular, intentional joy reduces the likelihood of behavioural and psychological failure points. A well-funded Joy bucket acts as a stabiliser. It doesn't replace the other buckets; it sustains them. Without it, growth becomes hollow, safety becomes neurotic, and essentials become burdensome.

Importantly, joy spending is not synonymous with frivolity. In fact, the most effective Joy buckets are deeply anchored in values. They are not about impulse but integrity—living in alignment with what truly matters. The irony is that many high-achievers, so skilled at defining metrics in their professional lives, never pause to define what joy means to them personally. They chase benchmarks and accolades but leave their inner life unbudgeted. And because the culture rewards this form of neglect with promotions, titles, and prestige, the misalignment compounds unnoticed—until the cost becomes unavoidable.

What does this look like in practice? Consider the high-income lawyer who budgets meticulously for retirement but hasn't seen close friends in months. Or the successful academic who lives on grants and deadlines but hasn't funded a weekend for solitude and reflection in five years. Or the startup founder who automates her investments monthly but treats a £50 concert ticket as an irresponsible extravagance. These are not outliers—they are archetypes. Their lives are full of output but thin on resonance. And eventually, the imbalance becomes unsustainable.

The antidote is not necessarily to spend more, but to *spend differently*. To treat joy not as an afterthought but as an asset class. Unlike equities or property, the ROI of joy isn't measured in percentages but in psychological dividends: motivation, creativity, resilience, relational depth. Research in behavioural economics has shown that individuals who make regular, small, intentional joy purchases report higher life satisfaction, stronger social bonds, and greater overall financial confidence. Not because they're spending more, but because they're *spending with purpose.*

This reframing is essential. A budget that includes joy is not a "soft" budget—it is a *complete* budget. It reflects the full range of what it means to be human, not just efficient. And the paradox is that when joy is budgeted, it becomes self-regulating. People who feel emotionally nourished are far less likely to engage in impulsive spending. They don't need to "blow off steam" with a last-minute getaway or "treat themselves" with another box of online deliveries. Their spending becomes a celebration of life, not a sedative for it.

There's also a broader economic insight at play. Joy spending has the potential to transform not just personal wellbeing but social fabric. When people allocate money to experiences, they tend to spend locally—on food, art, education, community. The ripple effects are real. A Joy bucket doesn't just circulate money; it deepens it. It anchors spending in identity and place, rather than algorithm and advertising. And for the individual, it offers a sense of *agency*—not just over their finances, but over their quality of life.

Still, there are practical tensions. What about debt? Should someone with credit card balances really budget for joy? The answer is not a blanket yes or no, but a recalibration. *Joy does not need to be expensive to be effective.* A £15 monthly "micro-joy" fund—used for books, coffee with a mentor, a subscription to an independent magazine—can yield disproportionate returns in morale and focus. The key is not the amount, but the intention. It is the *conscious claiming of space* for your own aliveness.

Of course, the concept of preventive joy challenges some deeply held beliefs. Particularly among those raised in scarcity or achievement cultures, there's a reflexive discomfort with pleasure that isn't "earned." But this discomfort is worth interrogating. Why must our joy be conditional? Who benefits from that arrangement? And how many people will delay joy until a point in life when their capacity to enjoy it has already diminished?

The most durable financial plans are those that don't rely on sustained deprivation. They work *because* they include joy—not despite it. This inclusion makes them livable, and therefore, repeatable. Budgeting becomes a way of honouring the present, not just securing the future. And this shift is subtle but radical: it places the human—not just the income—at the centre of the system.

The Joy bucket is the most neglected not because it lacks value, but because it lacks validation. Culture doesn't reward people for well-being; it rewards them for achievement. But a budget is not a trophy—it's a tool. And its success should be measured not only by what it builds in accounts, but by what it sustains in the person.

To fund joy is to assert that your emotional experience matters. That your life is not just a vehicle for goals, but a landscape for meaning. This doesn't require grand gestures. It requires integration. The Joy bucket, when used well, becomes the quiet foundation for a life that isn't just managed—but *felt*. And in a world that constantly tells you to optimise, that kind of presence is revolutionary.

Defining Joy on Your Terms

One of the more subtle financial missteps made by intelligent, high-functioning individuals is not overspending—but spending reflexively on things that yield no true joy. The distinction is not trivial. It marks the difference between money as a life-enhancing tool and money as a compensatory mechanism for stress, fatigue, or boredom. When we spend without intention, we do not just waste capital—we erode our sense of agency. Conversely, *spending that reflects your personal definition of joy becomes an act of self-knowledge and authorship*. And this, more than any budgeting app or frugality tip, is what gives financial strategy emotional integrity.

The central mistake in most approaches to joy spending is the failure to interrogate it. Joy is treated as either indulgence or reward—rarely as a form of deliberate expression. Yet the truth is that many expenses we categorise as "treats" are not joyful at all. They are habitual, numbing, obligatory, or socially scripted. That overpriced dinner you don't really enjoy. The monthly subscription you never use. The impulse purchase that seemed exciting but now sits untouched. These are not expressions of pleasure—they are financial inertia. *True joy is never passive.* It requires curation. It requires clarity. And above all, it requires self-definition.

This is where the concept of *intentional joy spending* becomes essential. Not all joy costs money. But when it does, the cost must be commensurate with meaning. That is: what you're paying should feel like a proportionate exchange for the depth or delight it brings. A £3 coffee savoured in solitude at a favourite café may be more nourishing than a £150 meal booked for obligation. A second-hand novel that ignites wonder may be worth more, emotionally, than the latest device you feel pressured to own. *The key is not to spend more, but to spend with sharper discernment.* What actually elevates your life? What lingers after the receipt is gone?

Start here: audit your spending through the lens of emotional return. Go through your last 90 days of discretionary expenses and ask, without defensiveness, what actually made you feel more alive, more connected, or more rested. Which purchases brought genuine satisfaction? Which were background noise? This is not a guilt exercise; it is a *diagnostic.* No one gets this perfectly right. But the mere act of asking resets the mental default from automatic consumption to deliberate selection.

Equally important is the practice of *reverse engineering joy.* Rather than asking "Can I afford this?", a more revealing question might be "Does this align with the kind of life I want to live?" Money is a directional force. If you never pause to define the coordinates, even high income won't lead to fulfilment. That holiday you keep postponing might not be about beaches or photos—it might be about giving yourself permission to rest. That concert ticket you hesitate over might not be about music—it might be about reconnecting with a part of yourself that your career has made you forget. *Joy spending is less about objects or events than it is about emotional reclamation.*

There is also a structural angle. Joy spending doesn't exist in a vacuum. It competes for space in a system often dominated by utility and prudence. The fear is that if you fund joy, you compromise goals. But the opposite is often true. *Well-placed joy acts as a pressure valve.* It allows for regular release, preventing the buildup of frustration that leads to financial blowouts—what psychologists call 'emotional depletion spending'. You see this when a diligent saver "snaps" and books a luxury escape they can't really afford. Not because they're irresponsible, but because they've starved a core human need for too long. The smarter approach is to design joy into the system. Not as a luxury, but as a stabiliser.

That means creating a *personal joy profile*—a working definition of what matters most to you emotionally, not just financially. For some, it may centre around beauty: design, art, nature. For others, it's about stimulation: travel, ideas, adventure. Others might crave intimacy: meals with loved ones, shared rituals, solitude with meaning. The clearer you are on your profile, the easier it becomes to filter spending choices through a lens of resonance. The goal is not to eliminate frivolity altogether—it is to differentiate between lightness that lifts and lightness that distracts.

There is a secondary insight here, too: *money is only one dimension of joy*. Many of the most sustaining pleasures cost nothing: a walk at the right time of day, a handwritten note, a recurring ritual that marks the week. But even these require intention. What we are resisting here is not materialism—it's mindlessness. There is no virtue in deprivation for its own sake. Nor is there virtue in abundance without clarity. The virtue lies in congruence: your spending matches your values, your personality, your season of life.

And yet many high-achievers struggle with this congruence. They are so accustomed to optimising for external goals—productivity, prestige, net worth—that they lose fluency in what actually makes them feel well. When asked what brings them joy, they falter. Not because they lack joy, but because they've never had to name it. This is where prompts can be powerful. Not to dictate joy, but to excavate it. Consider:

When did I last feel completely at ease, and what contributed to that feeling?

What small purchase in the past month made me feel seen, rested, or uplifted?

Are there any regular expenses that I resent or feel nothing toward?

If I had £100 to spend purely on joy, what would feel most worthwhile—right now, not in theory?

What experiences or things would I regret not giving myself permission to enjoy this year?

These are not budgetary questions. They are *self-alignment checks.* When used regularly, they keep your financial life emotionally tethered. They reveal not just what you buy, but who you are—and whether your money is serving that identity.

Let's also acknowledge the class dynamics embedded in joy. Culturally, we are trained to believe that joy is a reward for financial arrival. That once you reach a certain income tier, then you can "treat yourself." This logic is corrosive. It turns joy into a gate-kept commodity. It implies that dignity and delight must be postponed until you've proven yourself through earnings. But *joy is not post-capital reward—it is precondition to endurance.* This is especially vital for those in low-to-moderate income brackets, where life's pressures can be relentless. A modest Joy bucket, used well, can be a lifeline: an assertion of worth, of rhythm, of celebration amid strain.

In truth, *the most powerful form of financial intelligence is not accumulation—it is alignment.* The Joy bucket, when used with clarity, becomes a compass. It tells you whether your life is being lived or merely sustained. It sharpens the signal-to-noise ratio of your spending. And it restores pleasure to its rightful place—not as an escape, but as a dimension of strategy.

To define joy on your terms is not to sentimentalise money—it is to *humanise* it. To stop treating spending as either moral or immoral, and to start treating it as information. And in doing so, to reclaim something often lost in the logic of adult life: a sense that your days are not only purposeful, but beautiful—because you chose to make them so.

The Science of Anticipation and Memory

If you wanted to maximise the happiness you receive from a purchase, you wouldn't spend more—you'd spend differently. Not extravagantly, not impulsively, but *deliberately*, with attention to the temporal contours of joy: before, during, and after. Modern behavioural research tells us that the most enduring satisfaction from spending comes not from the grandeur of an item or experience, but from how it is anticipated, savoured, and remembered. In this sense, happiness is not purchased—it is constructed over time, through design. And yet most of us focus only on the moment of acquisition. We treat spending as a transaction, not a narrative. That is a mistake, not of ethics, but of missed opportunity.

Daniel Gilbert, a professor of psychology at Harvard, famously observed that humans are "anticipation machines." We derive pleasure not just from events themselves, but from *thinking about them in advance.*

Anticipation is not merely a prelude to joy—it is a form of joy itself, neurologically and emotionally. Studies using fMRI scans have shown that anticipating a rewarding event activates the same areas of the brain associated with experiencing the reward directly. The implication is profound: if you spread out small, meaningful joys across time, and allow yourself to anticipate them, *you effectively multiply your happiness without increasing your cost.*

Compare this to the impulsive purchase—a last-minute booking, a reactionary splurge, a rush of dopamine followed by a cognitive hangover. These tend to provide brief spikes of pleasure, quickly followed by hedonic adaptation. The brain, efficient as it is, recalibrates to the new normal with startling speed. That £400 handbag that thrilled on day one becomes just another accessory by week three. The expensive weekend escape loses its glow if it wasn't meaningfully anticipated or recalled. Impulse spending, in other words, burns hot and fast. *It satisfies a need for stimulation, not for fulfilment.*

Anticipation is not the only psychological lever. Memory plays a parallel role. Experiences that are encoded into lasting, vivid memory have a disproportionately high emotional return. The behavioural economist Dan Ariely found that *experiences gain in value the more they are revisited mentally*, even when the experience itself was not luxurious. A shared laugh, a view that stirred something wordless, a moment of quiet pride—these don't depreciate. In fact, they tend to *accrue emotional interest over time*. They are assets in the psychological sense, generating dividends of wellbeing long after the event.

This is why well-planned, intentional spending on joy doesn't just feel better—it *performs* better in emotional ROI terms. The key word here is *designed*. When you plan a joyful expenditure, you control the shape of the experience: you savour the build-up, you tune into the moment, and you integrate the memory afterward. This triptych—anticipation, experience, recollection—turns even a modest expense into a layered, meaningful event. You are not just "buying something nice." You are curating an arc of engagement with your own life.

There's also a counterintuitive insight worth noting: *less can be more, when it's spaced well*. Economists call this the principle of diminishing marginal utility, but it applies directly to joy. One well-planned experience, enjoyed in its full psychological arc, can outweigh five impulsive ones. A single dinner with friends, scheduled weeks in advance, marked on the calendar, discussed and dreamed about, might bring more total wellbeing than a month's worth of rushed takeaways and forgettable indulgences. The latter may fill time, but the former fills memory.

Why, then, do people default to the impulse path? In part, because it's easier. Our modern environment trains us for immediacy: same-day delivery, one-click gratification, algorithmic nudges. There is little friction to help us pause. But *ease is not the same as depth*. Thoughtful joy requires resistance to the current. It asks you to *want with intention,* not just respond to stimuli. It's a quiet rebellion against the logic of the marketplace, which profits from your forgetfulness and habituation.

From a practical standpoint, this insight suggests a simple but powerful financial shift: allocate your Joy budget not only by category, but by *timing*. Think of joy in quarters, in weeks, in seasons. Pre-book meaningful experiences and mark them visibly in your calendar. Send yourself reminders. Build in the savour. For example, if you love live music, choose one or two concerts per quarter, and let the anticipation stretch out. If you enjoy short solo retreats, block one weekend every few months, and start imagining the details in advance. The structure isn't restrictive—it's amplifying. *Planning becomes part of the pleasure.*

Equally, it's worth noting that certain types of spending *generate more durable memories* than others. Experiences tend to outperform material goods in this regard. A landmark study by Thomas Gilovich at Cornell University found that experiences, even when less objectively valuable, tend to be more closely tied to identity, shared meaning, and long-term happiness. People don't relive the day they bought a new phone—they relive the moment they hiked to a lookout with a friend or took their child to the theatre for the first time. *Memory is not a passive archive—it's an active currency.*

There's a practical application here for anyone designing a Joy bucket: curate not just what you spend on, but *how it will be remembered*. Ask yourself: will I talk about this five years from now? Will I share it with someone? Will it matter to who I am? The answer doesn't have to be profound. A quiet Sunday ritual can be as meaningful as a grand holiday, if it reflects something true. What matters is the resonance—not the price.

Another dimension of anticipation is its effect on resilience. Psychologists have found that having something to look forward to *buffers against current stress*. When life feels uncertain or overwhelming, even a small beacon on the horizon can stabilise mood, improve decision-making, and offer emotional continuity. A planned afternoon off, a walk with a friend, a night of cooking something indulgent—these are not trivialities. They are *psychological handrails*, especially in high-pressure seasons. To invest in anticipation is to *invest in future you*.

Yet none of this negates spontaneity. The goal is not to turn joy into another productivity metric. Some of life's richest pleasures arrive unplanned. But the discipline of anticipating joy does not eliminate spontaneity—it protects it. By designing space for joy, you create bandwidth for surprise. You prevent joy from becoming a casualty of exhaustion. And when spontaneous joy *does* arise, it lands on a more receptive, less depleted self.

There is a final, philosophical point: *the way we design joy reflects the way we value time*. Anyone can spend money. But to curate anticipation and memory is to engage with your life as a temporal experience, not just a logistical one. It is to respect the unfolding of your days. And it is to say, in practical terms, that *your happiness is worth structuring for*—

not later, not in retirement, but now, in rhythm with your current reality.

If the purpose of a Joy bucket is not just escape, but enhancement, then this science offers a blueprint. Prioritise anticipation. Honour memory. Spend not for the rush, but for the resonance. And in doing so, turn joy from a fleeting feeling into a *practised art*.

Joy Is Not Just for the Rich

It is a damaging misconception that joy must be postponed until financial prosperity arrives. That pleasure, leisure, and emotional nourishment are luxuries reserved for those who have "earned" them in economic terms. But across communities, time zones, and pay brackets, this belief proves to be not only false, but destructive. When the architecture of personal finance is constructed without space for joy, it slowly erodes the human spirit. And when budgeting philosophies frame joy as indulgence rather than necessity, they fail not only morally, but strategically.

Joy is not a financial reward. It is a stabilising input. For people living on limited incomes, especially, joy becomes a protective force—something that nourishes identity, sustains relationships, and counterbalances stress. Far from being frivolous, this kind of spending plays a vital role in mental and social resilience. The idea that it must be deferred until one is "rich enough" to deserve it not only misreads human psychology, but reinforces an unhealthy binary: necessity versus luxury. The truth is more nuanced.

In many cases, what looks like a small indulgence is, in fact, a quiet declaration of dignity.

Take the example of Anika, a single mother in Birmingham earning just under £26,000 per year working in early childhood education. Her income barely stretches across essentials, rent, and modest savings. But every other Saturday, she hosts a "family cinema night" in her living room: popcorn made from kernels, blankets on the floor, a film preselected from free streaming options. She spends under £5. Yet the event is ritualised, anticipated, and loved by her two sons. "It makes the week feel like it has a peak," she explains. "Otherwise, you're just surviving. This gives us something to *live for,* not just *get through*." The significance of that ritual isn't in the cost—it's in the continuity. It's a deliberately carved-out moment of joy, created within a tight budget, but rich in emotional return.

Contrast this with the dominant messaging in mainstream financial advice. Popular budgeting apps often categorise any entertainment, dining, or personal care as "discretionary." These are the first items encouraged to be slashed. But for people in high-stress, low-autonomy roles—nurses, service workers, carers—these "discretionary" expenses often represent their only expressions of autonomy. A meal out with a friend, a fresh haircut before a job interview, or a small gift for a child's birthday is not excess. *It is participation in life.* To treat it as unnecessary is to ignore the psychological and cultural contexts in which people make meaning.

It's also worth acknowledging that joy spending, when done intentionally, often *improves* financial behaviour elsewhere. A compelling study from the University of Michigan found that low-income individuals who were given a small "fun budget" alongside their basic needs subsidy reported higher satisfaction *and* more disciplined spending in other areas. Why? Because they didn't feel deprived. They didn't need to rebel against an austerity model. *Moderate, structured joy reduces the likelihood of impulsive, destructive spending.* It turns out that joy is not the enemy of discipline—it's a precondition for it.

Consider Marcus, a part-time warehouse worker in Leeds who earns just under the national minimum wage. Every month, he sets aside £10—not more—for a ritual he calls his "record shop hour." He takes a walk to a local second-hand vinyl store, browses, and usually buys one used record. "It's not about the music," he admits. "It's about the act of choosing something. Feeling like I can still decide how to live." That £10 could, in theory, go toward bills. But Marcus knows that without it, his sense of agency erodes. His record habit isn't about consumption—it's about continuity of self.

The mechanics of joy spending are not defined by income. They are defined by *intention*. Whether you're earning £1,200 or £12,000 a month, the question is the same: *What spending patterns help you feel most alive?* Not what looks good on paper, not what impresses others, but what affirms who you are. For lower-income earners, the challenge is often that this space feels culturally illegitimate. They are praised for being frugal, admired for self-sacrifice, and subtly shamed for any visible pleasure. Yet no one thrives on martyrdom. Even the most pragmatic budgeting system must make room for the soul.

This is where the 5-Bucket model proves its relevance. By explicitly allocating space for Joy as a legitimate category, it resists the moralism of austerity. It formalises what is often relegated to guilt. And in doing so, it empowers people across income levels to spend joyfully *without shame.* For someone living close to the financial edge, seeing Joy as a valid allocation—however small—can be transformational. It reclaims a portion of money as something more than survival fuel. It becomes a tool for expression, for connection, for memory-making.

It is also vital to redefine what counts as joy spending. It doesn't need to be flamboyant. In fact, the most resonant forms of joy are often quiet, modest, and context-specific. A taxi ride that allows a parent to attend a child's performance after a double shift. A new shirt for a religious festival. A coffee shared with a friend who understands your world. These are not indulgences. *They are acts of preservation.* And they deserve to be recognised as such.

Social scientists have long acknowledged that relative deprivation—not absolute poverty—is what drives much of the psychological distress around money. When people feel they are excluded from ordinary rituals of celebration or connection, they internalise failure. Joy spending disrupts this narrative. It creates moments where people can *participate fully in life*, even if only for an hour or a day. And in doing so, it reasserts a basic truth: everyone deserves beauty, dignity, and rest.

Of course, the danger lies in extremes. If joy spending becomes escapist or compensatory—masking deeper structural or emotional needs—it can destabilise. But the solution is not to eliminate joy. It is to *make it conscious*. When people on low incomes engage in premeditated, small-scale joy spending, it often signals *high financial intelligence*. They know their constraints. They choose wisely. They invest not just in needs, but in morale.

There is also a community angle. Joy, when shared, magnifies. In low-income neighbourhoods, communal joy often substitutes for individual luxury. Potluck dinners, group walks, music in public parks, community arts events—these are not lesser versions of elite experiences. They are a *different economy of joy*, one based on accessibility, participation, and relational richness. When we treat these as second-tier, we reveal the class bias baked into most financial discourse. But when we validate and celebrate them, we broaden the spectrum of what wealth looks like.

It's not a coincidence that some of the world's most joy-rich cultures are not its wealthiest. From rural villages in Southeast Asia to immigrant enclaves in European cities, you find practices of celebration, of ritualised leisure, of adornment and beauty—all maintained with ingenuity and care, not affluence. The financial world could learn something from this: *sustainable joy is a design problem, not a purchasing power issue.*

In practical terms, budgeting for joy on a low income requires clarity, not capital. The question is not, "Can I afford something extravagant?" but "What modest, meaningful ritual can I build into my life this month?" It could be £5 or £50. What matters is that it's deliberate. That it is protected from guilt. That it is recognised not as leakage, but as leverage. Because a joyful person is more likely to stay resilient. More likely to think long-term. More likely to resist the psychological spiral of scarcity.

To exclude joy from financial systems is not just an oversight—it is a form of poverty-thinking, even among the affluent. When we understand that joy is not a reward for wealth but a foundation for it, we build healthier, more humane financial architectures. And when we affirm that joy belongs to everyone, regardless of income, we extend dignity where it has too often been denied.

Joy is not just for the rich. It never was. But recognising this truth, and building for it, is a radical act of financial intelligence.

Chapter 7
Overflow—Your Financial Weather Vane

Every financial system, no matter how carefully constructed, generates noise. But not all noise is meaningless. Some of it carries signal—subtle cues about alignment, drift, or discipline. Overflow, in this sense, is never just leftover money. It is not merely the residue of efficiency, nor a discretionary fund for play. It is diagnostic. How you handle overflow, and perhaps more importantly, what it reveals, reflects the sophistication and adaptability of your financial life. If budgeting is about structure, overflow is about interpretation—it transforms a static protocol into a living, responsive loop.

This chapter invites a reframing: overflow should be treated not as bonus or indulgence, but as data. Traditional thinking often casts leftover funds as either reward or proof of virtue, a gold star for restraint. Yet such interpretations are superficial. Surplus does not automatically indicate efficiency; sometimes it signals neglect, under-investment, or emotional disengagement. Conversely, the absence of overflow isn't necessarily alarming—if every penny has been allocated deliberately, a zero balance may speak to precision rather than scarcity. Overflow is less about quantity than about meaning.

Imagine an aircraft's fuel gauge. A novice might rejoice at a surplus. An experienced pilot, however, questions it: is this efficiency, or have we taken the wrong route? Did we bypass something requiring attention? Surplus in financial life is rarely neutral; it tells a story. The skill lies in learning to read it.

Within the five-bucket framework—Needs, Safety, Joy, Growth, and Overflow—once the essential buckets are consistently funded, any remaining funds in Overflow become a live indicator of system performance. Too little might suggest creeping fixed costs; too much might indicate that high-leverage areas like Joy or Growth are being starved out of reflexive frugality. In either case, it is not the volume of Overflow that matters, but the conversation it sparks.

The concept becomes even more critical with irregular income. Freelancers, gig workers, and others who experience episodic surges—project payouts, tax refunds, or bonuses—often mishandle these inflows. Not due to recklessness, but because they lack clarity: what is this money, and what should I do with it? The five-bucket system addresses this not through rigid percentages, but by offering a decision map, assigning funds based on optimal use rather than origin.

It is essential to distinguish overflow from leakage. Both involve money leaving the structured system, yet their implications diverge sharply. Leakage is unconscious—spending driven by impulse, fatigue, or emotional friction. Overflow is deliberate—residual money after all buckets are intentionally funded. They feel alike in the moment, yet their downstream effects differ profoundly. Ignoring this distinction blinds one to the true performance of a financial engine.

Overflow is more than diagnostic; it is directional. Behavioural finance introduces the notion of "slack"—unallocated mental or material bandwidth for adaptability. Overflow is financial slack. Unlike psychological slack, which may sit unused, financial overflow can be deployed strategically: into Safety when risks rise, into Growth when opportunity emerges, or into Joy when emotional reserves wane. It functions as an opportunity scanner, signalling where momentum can be pursued and providing the means to do so.

Consider Leila, a young urban planner in Manchester. Her salary is stable, yet in recent months, she notices growing overflow. Initially, pride bubbles up. But a closer inspection reveals the source: she has been underfunding Joy, skipping social rituals and personal indulgences to conserve costs. Her overflow isn't optimisation—it is silent depletion. Recognising this, she doesn't merely reroute funds; she recalibrates values. Monthly creative workshops return to her schedule, along with Saturday café visits—modest expenditures with high emotional yield. Overflow has delivered not just money, but insight.

The Overflow bucket is a feedback loop, not a reward pile. It demands interrogation, not indulgence. Are you growing efficiency or drifting emotionally? Is life expanding or constricting? Are trade-offs conscious, or are you coasting? Overflow functions like lab results—objective, empirical, brimming with insight, if interpreted correctly.

Windfalls illustrate the psychological nuance further. Sudden, unplanned income often distorts valuation logic. Behavioural economists term this "mental accounting bias": the tendency to treat money differently based on origin. A

£1,000 tax refund feels distinct from £1,000 earned through overtime, despite identical value. Windfalls frequently justify impulsive spending, simply because the money lacks defined purpose. The five-bucket approach mitigates this, filtering every pound through consistent values, irrespective of source.

Allocation differs from automation. Overflow decisions resist rules-of-thumb; they require deliberate attention. Each surplus is a diagnostic touchpoint: a signal that warrants the question, "What's changed?" Larger-than-normal overflow may suggest an early investment opportunity, a lifestyle adjustment, or a misalignment in fixed costs—or it may indicate nothing at all, simply reflecting a system accumulating agility. The answer emerges only through attentive interpretation.

Overflow also performs psychological repair. Extended financial strain—debts, underemployment, instability—can make surplus destabilising. Instead of relief, it provokes guilt or pressure: Should I invest, save, spend? In such contexts, the most intelligent use may be ease—spending not to optimise, but to recalibrate. A meal with a friend, a spontaneous train ride, an unstructured day. These are not frivolous; they are decompression, preventing systemic damage.

In mature systems, overflow evolves from reactive to proactive. It tests ideas, hedges experiments, expresses values not yet fully funded by the main budget. It can co-fund a friend's project, support a cause, seed a venture, or enable a short sabbatical—all without compromising core operations. Overflow is not icing; it is the laboratory. Without it, budgets calcify; with it, they remain dynamic. It is the curiosity budget—the space to explore what lies beyond routine.

Overflow's presence does not automatically signal success, nor does its absence indicate failure. Both are metrics, and their significance lies in interpretation. Overflow invites reflection: on habits, alignment, and lived financial experience. It encourages nuance over narrative, precision over pride, dialogue over default.

This chapter is not a manual for "what to do" with surplus. It is about recognising overflow as a signal, not a side effect. It is not an end in itself, but a tool. Mastering it offers insight not merely into the state of your finances, but into the direction of your life.

Where the Leftover Money Goes

There is an instinctive relief many people feel when they see unspent money accumulating at the end of a month. Whether it's £40 or £400, the presence of leftover funds evokes a comforting sense of control—proof, it seems, that you're "doing something right." But while surplus money may suggest prudence on the surface, the question rarely asked is *what exactly is this money saying?* Surplus is not inherently virtuous. It is not automatically efficient, and it is certainly not silent. In the five-bucket model, overflow is not a prize. It is a *metric,* and one that requires close inspection. The presence of overflow is not about indulgence—it's about *clarity*. Interpreting it correctly is one of the most underutilised skills in personal finance.

One of the most dangerous misreadings in budgeting is the belief that leftover money always represents good financial behaviour. In truth, it can represent almost anything: excessive caution, emotional disengagement, neglected needs, delayed decision-making, or deferred self-care. Overflow is multivalent. It needs context to be understood. If your Needs, Safety, Joy, and Growth buckets are underfunded—either slightly or significantly—then overflow may signal avoidance or misalignment rather than mastery. Surplus can just as easily be a sign of internal austerity as it can be of external abundance. Without interpretation, it is meaningless. With interpretation, it becomes a window into how well your values and actions are actually synchronising.

To view overflow as surplus alone is to flatten its complexity. Leftover money is not simply "what's left." It is often what's *unaddressed*. Take the case of Raj, a mid-level engineer in his late thirties, living in Leeds. After applying the five-bucket system for three months, Raj noticed an increasing amount building in his Overflow bucket. At first, he was pleased. But when reviewing his allocations, he realised he had been consistently underfunding his Joy bucket—missing opportunities to connect with friends, skipping concerts he once loved, and holding off on a long-desired cycling trip. The excess in Overflow wasn't optimisation—it was omission. His budget was technically working, but it wasn't *alive*. Raj rebalanced, shifting some funds from Overflow back into Joy. The result was not just more satisfaction, but more *balance*—and a sense that his financial behaviour was aligned with the life he actually wanted to live.

This is the interpretive leap many systems lack. Standard budgeting frameworks tend to present leftover money as a win—something to invest, save, or reward oneself with. The implication is that all essential categories have been met and what remains is free. But this model assumes the budget itself is perfectly constructed. It assumes all needs have been consciously addressed and that none have been minimised for the sake of efficiency. In reality, many people under-allocate for Joy or Safety, either because they haven't articulated what those buckets mean in their context, or because they conflate frugality with virtue. *Financial frugality without emotional congruence is simply deprivation in disguise.*

Overflow should be read as feedback. Is your system too rigid? Are your assumptions outdated? Has your lifestyle changed but your allocations have not? Is your risk profile different from when you first set your Safety contributions? These questions aren't just theoretical—they're diagnostic. For instance, consider a family in Edinburgh whose monthly Overflow increased sharply after they paid off their car loan. Rather than immediately reallocating those funds to Growth or discretionary spending, they examined their household routines. They realised that their Joy bucket—especially around shared family experiences—had been undernourished during the repayment period. Instead of redirecting the money to "future gains," they enhanced the present, scheduling regular family outings and occasional overnight trips. The overflow, rather than being siphoned into an abstract savings goal, was used to *rebuild connective tissue.*

A mature financial system does not treat overflow as spare change. It treats it as a *report card.* A drop in overflow doesn't necessarily signal overspending—it may indicate a rebalancing effort, a medical emergency, or a seasonal spike in Joy expenses. An increase doesn't necessarily mean optimisation—it may mean unnoticed underfunding. This is where behavioural awareness becomes crucial. Instead of chasing overflow as a target or disregarding it as a bonus, financially literate individuals ask a better question: *What is this number telling me about the life I am—or am not—living?*

This reframing is particularly important in cultures and households where money is tightly associated with discipline, self-restraint, or guilt. In such environments, any leftover money is treated with reverence. It becomes sacrosanct. The danger here is not overspending but emotional rigidity. The five-bucket system is designed to ensure every pound has a purpose, not a pedestal. If that purpose is evolving—if Joy needs more room, if Growth opportunities arise, if Safety thresholds shift—then overflow is the buffer that allows *intentional responsiveness*.

Behavioural finance also provides insight into how people misread surplus. Studies in mental accounting have shown that individuals are more likely to allocate "extra" funds—

bonuses, rebates, unspent budget—to hedonic or impulsive categories. This is not inherently wrong. But it often occurs *without awareness*. The money feels looser, so the discipline softens. What makes the five-bucket model unique is that it does not privilege the origin of money. Every pound—earned, found, gifted, refunded—passes through the same logic. What bucket needs this most *right now*?

That question is especially vital during moments of life transition. Consider Lucy, a graphic designer in Glasgow, who received a modest inheritance. She could have defaulted to paying off her mortgage, or investing it blindly, or splurging. Instead, she used the five-bucket lens to interpret what the money could do. Part went to bolster her Safety bucket—she increased her insurance coverage and created a longer-term emergency buffer. Some went into Growth, funding a skills course she had put off for years. And critically, she expanded her Joy bucket, allowing space for travel and family connection she had long postponed. Her Overflow didn't become a question mark—it became a *clarifying lens*.

To treat leftover money as a passive category is to abdicate one of the most insightful functions of budgeting. Overflow is not an accident—it is a metric of alignment. It is the space where intention meets reality. But like any signal, it must be *interpreted*. A growing Overflow bucket may be applauded too quickly. A shrinking one may trigger fear unnecessarily. Both reactions are incomplete. What matters is not the size of the surplus, but its meaning relative to the rest of your system.

When properly understood, overflow enables course correction. It reveals trends before they become problems. It surfaces hidden sacrifices. It spotlights unconscious inertia. And crucially, it gives you *room*—room to experiment, to adjust, to reconnect with your actual preferences rather than your automatic habits. Overflow, then, becomes more than a category. It becomes a literacy. A signal. Not of how much is left—but of how well you are *listening*.

Detecting Drift or Discipline

One of the most misunderstood signals in personal finance is the presence—or absence—of leftover money. It seems innocuous at first. A little more at the end of the month? Good. A little less? Tighten up. But beneath that binary reaction lies a more revealing question: *What is this pattern telling me about the structural integrity of my financial system?* Overflow, viewed through the right lens, is a diagnostic tool. Not a prize for good behaviour, nor a penalty for indulgence. It is neither applause nor alarm—it is data. And the pattern it forms over time, when properly interpreted, offers a window into whether your spending system is functioning with discipline or quietly drifting off course.

Drift is insidious because it often arrives masked as routine. Habits form, preferences shift, and small irregularities accumulate. There is no dramatic change, no crisis. Just a gradual erosion of alignment between your actual values and your financial expressions of them. And unless you are actively observing the movement of overflow—month by month, context by context—drift will masquerade as discipline. That is the paradox. *True financial discipline requires more than consistency. It requires attunement.*

Consider the case of Elaine, a self-employed translator based in Bristol. When she first implemented the five-bucket system, her Overflow bucket sat at a steady £150 each month. For a while, this seemed ideal—evidence that her system was neither overextended nor excessively tight. But as her workload increased, she began spending less on Joy, skipping her weekly ceramics class and deferring social outings. The Overflow bucket swelled, quietly, to £300. Then £450. On paper, she was "saving" more. But in reality, her underfunded Joy bucket was a symptom of burnout waiting to happen. The system hadn't failed. *She had stopped listening to what it was telling her.* The drift was slow, but it was real—and it masked itself as good discipline.

This is why patterns matter more than points. A single month's surplus or deficit says almost nothing. But three months of surplus with a shrinking Joy or Safety allocation? That's not success. That's likely unexamined tension. Equally, if overflow diminishes steadily without any increase in bucket contributions—or any memorable upgrades to lived experience—then it may be signalling silent leakage. Subscriptions left to auto-renew. Incremental lifestyle creep. Unplanned generosity without rebalancing. These aren't emergencies, but they are distortions. Left unchecked, they calcify into habits that drain clarity from your system. *When overflow patterns change, the system is trying to speak. The question is whether you're tuned in or tuned out.*

It's easy to mistake suppression for strength. High achievers often pride themselves on unspent funds, on staying "under budget," as if restraint were an end in itself. But financial health is not about hoarding surplus. It's about aligning your money with your life's actual demands and desires. If overflow is rising while important categories remain unaddressed, the question is not "How do I use this surplus?" but rather, *"Why is it there in the first place?"* What need or desire has been ignored, deferred, or miscalculated? Sometimes the answer is joyful—perhaps a planned reduction in housing costs has freed up capacity. But often, it's more subtle: social withdrawal, postponed self-care, or risk aversion masquerading as frugality.

Discipline, properly defined, is not about austerity. It is about fidelity to your priorities. A well-calibrated system should generate surplus as a by-product of alignment—not as its central aim. If overflow is growing because you are funding your Growth, Safety, and Joy buckets with precision and still have breathing room, *that is discipline*. But if overflow is growing because you haven't recalibrated your categories in nine months and are operating on outdated assumptions, *that is drift with a false halo*. And therein lies the importance of active interpretation.

Behavioural science adds a layer of complexity here. People are notoriously bad at noticing slow changes. The psychology of habituation means we become less responsive to incremental shifts over time—whether in weight, mood, or money. We normalise the new baseline quickly. A creeping subscription cost becomes part of the mental wallpaper. A skipped holiday feels like a responsible trade-off until emotional fatigue sets in. *Drift is not dramatic by nature—but its effects compound quietly, making the system feel brittle before anyone sounds the alarm.*

The solution is not hyper-vigilance. It is *structured reflection*. A monthly or quarterly review of overflow patterns—against the backdrop of your lived reality—is often enough. The goal is not to make overflow predictable; it is to make it *interpretable*. For instance, if you receive a windfall—say, a tax refund—and overflow spikes for that month, no concern. But if your baseline spending has crept upward and overflow vanishes despite stable income, the drift is likely internal. You're spending more *by default*, not by design.

One effective practice is tracking variance alongside narrative. That is: don't just record how much overflow exists. Document *why* you think it exists. Was there a major expense that month? Did you reduce your Joy spending because of travel or illness? Did you skip your usual discretionary activities without realising the cost to morale? These annotations help make the system legible. Because financial patterns without personal context are just numbers. *Meaning lives in the margin notes.*

Take James and Linh, a couple in Manchester who share a joint five-bucket budget. For several months, their Overflow hovered near zero. Initially concerned, they examined their allocations and found no shortfalls. What changed, however, was their Joy and Growth buckets: both had been proactively increased as they began attending workshops, investing in therapy, and travelling more intentionally. The reduced overflow wasn't failure—it was *precision*. Their spending system wasn't leaking. It was *working exactly as designed*, optimising for fulfilment rather than leftover cash.

This is the nuance. Overflow can shrink for healthy reasons—or for subtle, corrosive ones. It can grow as a sign of evolving alignment—or of unintended constraint. There is no universal threshold, no right number. What matters is *pattern literacy*. Are your surpluses matching your surplus energy? Are your shortages aligned with deliberate reinvestment elsewhere? Or are these movements unconscious, erratic, or driven by fatigue, inertia, or social pressure?

Drift isn't just financial. It is psychological. It's what happens when life changes and your system doesn't. It's what accrues when you keep telling yourself you'll adjust things "next month." And eventually, the signals get buried under routine. But discipline—the real kind—is not about resisting change. It's about recognising it early enough to respond intelligently. The five-bucket framework gives you that lens. But it does not automate awareness. *Interpretation is your responsibility. Discipline is your practice. And drift is always the risk that rides in silence unless you ask the right questions.*

Done well, this act of financial inquiry transforms overflow from an afterthought into a forecasting tool. It tells you, with subtlety, whether your map still fits the territory. It helps you spot when restraint is slipping toward neglect or when generosity is tipping into imbalance. Most importantly, it gives you the opportunity to *course-correct before compromise becomes collapse.* That is not just budgeting. That is strategy. That is stewardship. And that, ultimately, is the discipline worth cultivating.

Windfalls, Bonuses, and Tax Refunds

There is a particular psychological tension embedded in sudden income: the momentary illusion that it changes everything. A bonus lands. A tax refund arrives. An unexpected inheritance or client overpayment appears in the account. Rationally, the numbers may pale in comparison to one's annual earnings. But emotionally, irregular income feels expansive. It exists outside the constraints of the regular budget, free from the usual tug-of-war between bills and goals. And this perceived freedom—if not managed within a disciplined structure—often breeds one of two outcomes: either it dissipates in a blur of impulse, or it gets hoarded with a vague sense of guilt. Neither is optimal. *Windfalls should not be treated as emotional escape valves, nor as sacred funds we dare not touch. They should be interpreted.*

The five-bucket model offers a practical lens for doing precisely that. It enables the reclassification of windfalls from disruptive events into calibrated financial signals—opportunities to re-align, not destabilise. Because when viewed correctly, a sudden influx of funds does not represent surplus. It represents *choice*. And that choice should not default to indulgence or restraint. It should default to *intentionality*.

The first error most people make with windfalls is to think of them as distinct from the rest of their financial ecosystem. A tax refund, for instance, is often seen as a "freebie"—a reward rather than a correction. But in most cases, a refund merely reflects an overpayment throughout the year. That money was always yours; you just gave the government an interest-free loan. Framing it as a bonus distorts its role and warps the spending psychology that follows. The same holds true for end-of-year employer bonuses, which are frequently linked more to performance reviews than to planning. These funds, if integrated carefully into your existing system, can amplify its integrity. But if treated as exceptional, they risk introducing volatility into otherwise stable spending rhythms.

One of the clearest examples comes from Raj, a London-based UX designer who received a £5,000 year-end bonus. Historically, his approach had been to split such windfalls arbitrarily: a holiday, some tech upgrades, the rest into savings. But after adopting the five-bucket model, he approached the bonus as *fluid income,* not discretionary frosting. He began by asking a foundational question: *Which buckets are currently under strain?* His Joy bucket had been neglected for months due to project stress. His Growth bucket, which he had hoped to use for a part-time coding course, was underfunded. His Safety bucket was robust, and Overflow had been modest but stable. Based on this real-time diagnostic, he allocated £1,200 to Growth, £800 to Joy, added £1,000 to Safety as a conservative buffer, and left £2,000 in Overflow to observe whether any rebalancing would be needed in the coming quarter. No grand indulgence. No punitive austerity. Just clarity, applied to a one-time event.

This is the key: *The utility of a windfall is maximised when it is interpreted through your system—not when it dictates the system's exception.* Regular income structures should remain intact. You do not rewrite your budget because your employer decided to be generous. You interpret the event as a variable input into a stable frame. That's how you avoid the volatility trap, where one good month triggers a new lifestyle baseline and every subsequent "normal" month feels like deprivation.

Behavioural economics reinforces this tension. Research on mental accounting shows that people tend to assign different emotional values to money based on its origin. "Found money" feels more expendable. Casino winnings, birthday gifts, tax refunds—these are treated as qualitatively different from earned salary, even when numerically identical. This bias—sometimes useful, often dangerous—explains why the same person might agonise over a £300 expense from their paycheck but spend a £500 refund with minimal scrutiny. The five-bucket model counters this psychological asymmetry by *neutralising the emotional weight of money's origin*. In this framework, all income—regular or not—is filtered through the same categories. What changes is *where the friction is felt*. A windfall doesn't go into a separate emotional bucket; it flows through the same pipes and is shaped by the same priorities.

There's also a cultural dimension to consider. In many professional environments, bonuses are both opaque and socially charged. Employees often learn about each other's bonuses anecdotally, leading to comparison, resentment, or overcompensation. Within families, sudden income events can trigger expectation dynamics—gifts to others, financial support, or shared expenditures that go unplanned. Without a clearly defined allocation model, these moments invite conflict or confusion. A transparent five-bucket plan does more than distribute funds. It *prevents friction*. It creates language for explaining how you use irregular income, which in turn makes you less vulnerable to guilt, pressure, or ambiguity.

Some might argue that windfalls are the very moments when budgeting should be suspended—that it is precisely because the money is unexpected that it should be used freely. But this logic misframes freedom. *True financial freedom is not the absence of structure. It is the presence of choice, exercised within a frame you trust.* A windfall offers a high-stakes opportunity to test the fidelity of your system. If you feel suffocated by the idea of allocating a £10,000 inheritance through your buckets, the problem is not the model. It's your relationship to it. Is it too rigid? Have your categories stopped reflecting your life? Or are you hoping that a sudden influx of cash will somehow absolve you of the responsibility to decide wisely?

The reality is that windfalls tend to reveal more about your system than they disrupt it. A person with unclear priorities will use a tax refund as a buffer against indecision. A person with a disciplined, responsive system will use the same refund to make precise, intentional moves—either shoring up underfunded areas or testing new allocations based on emergent values.

Consider Lena, a single mother in Birmingham who received a £3,500 redundancy payout after a voluntary exit from her job. The money came at a vulnerable moment. Her instinct was to stash it all into savings. But when she reviewed her five buckets, she noticed that her Safety fund already covered five months of expenses. Her Growth bucket, however, was non-existent—and she had long wanted to retrain as a dental hygienist. She allocated £2,000 to enrol in a part-time course and set aside £1,000 for Joy-related activities with her son—weekend trips, museum passes, and a long-postponed camping holiday. The remaining £500 went to Overflow, which later helped her recalibrate monthly costs as she transitioned into freelance work. This was not indulgence. It was *strategic reallocation* in response to a rare but powerful income event.

Irregular income requires calm, not celebration. The stakes are high precisely because these events are infrequent. A windfall mishandled does more than waste money—it *erodes trust in your own system.* It teaches your nervous system that stability is conditional, that large inputs cause chaos. And over time, this erodes not just financial health but personal confidence. The antidote is not constraint. It is *coherence.* Treat the windfall not as a reward, but as a prompt: What now needs rebalancing? What future commitment can be funded in advance? What blind spot has capacity revealed?

In the five-bucket model, windfalls are not wildcards. They are pressure tests. They allow for accelerated rebalancing, deeper insight into category friction, and targeted recalibration. They give you the rare luxury of decision-making without immediate consequence—a financial dress rehearsal for a more flexible future. But only if you treat them as part of the system. Not as a break from it.

The next time you receive unexpected income—whether it's £200 from a forgotten rebate or £20,000 from an inheritance—don't rush to assign it moral weight. Pause. Breathe. Then bring it to the table of your system, and ask the only question that matters: *What will serve the whole?*

Because windfalls, like water, will flow wherever there's space. The art is in deciding *which space truly needs it.*

Overflow as Opportunity Scanner

Excess funds tend to seduce with their ambiguity. They sit unassigned, unattached, waiting to be shaped by whatever story the moment offers. Some see overflow as a reward—disposable and unexamined. Others treat it with suspicion, fearing to move it lest they "do the wrong thing." But in a functional, responsive budgeting model, overflow isn't merely the remainder. *It is diagnostic.* It tells you what has changed, what is misaligned, what deserves reinforcement or redistribution. Properly observed, it becomes a kind of financial sonar—detecting shifts in your needs, habits, values, and external conditions before they become problems or missed opportunities.

Most people treat budgeting as a static act. Set the categories, allocate the amounts, rinse, repeat. But financial life is dynamic, subject to the push and pull of family needs, professional demands, economic shifts, and personal evolution. A budget that cannot interpret its own overflow is like a compass with no needle—it might look orderly, but it's directionless. *Overflow is not surplus. It is signal.* It indicates either over-allocation, behavioural change, improved efficiency, or unacknowledged drift. The only mistake is failing to ask what it's pointing to.

Consider the case of Marcia, a freelance copyeditor in Manchester. After several months of stable income and consistent outflows, she noticed a monthly overflow that averaged £600—more than usual. She hadn't changed her lifestyle, or so she thought. But after a closer audit, she realised that her children had transitioned from costly after-school care to free community programmes. At the same time, she had reduced her weekly takeaway habit without noticing, largely due to a new interest in home cooking. The overflow wasn't a gift; it was a mirror. It reflected a shift in both spending and values. Rather than automatically increasing her discretionary budget, Marcia used the signal to rebalance: she redirected £200 monthly into her Growth bucket for a business writing course and added £100 to Joy, earmarked for future travel with her family. The remaining £300 she left in Overflow for three months to observe whether the pattern held. It did. By the end of the year, she'd upskilled, travelled more meaningfully, and maintained budgetary resilience—all without a single raise.

This is the difference between accidental surplus and intentional scanning. *Overflow interpreted with rigour allows you to notice the silent wins of frugality, habit shifts, or economic change—and to reinvest them deliberately.* Rather than letting good fortune leak into lifestyle inflation, it becomes raw material for strategic recalibration.

The principle becomes even more vital during periods of inflation or economic uncertainty. When costs are rising, overflow shrinks—or disappears entirely. If your overflow has quietly evaporated over three consecutive months, that's not a budgeting fluke. It's a sign that your fixed allocations may be under pressure. Something in the system has changed, and the model is no longer fully aligned with the real world. *The absence of overflow can be as revealing as its presence.* In fact, a disappearing overflow is often the first visible evidence of lifestyle creep, undiagnosed inflation, or overconfidence in variable spending.

This is why treating overflow as "extra" is fundamentally flawed. It trains the brain to treat the margin as a treat. But in financial systems thinking, margins are data-rich. They hold early indicators of systemic drift—positive or negative. Ignoring them is like ignoring the warning lights on a dashboard because the car still runs. *Disciplined systems don't just account for overflow; they interrogate it.*

There is also a behavioural benefit to scanning overflow regularly. When you examine excess funds not from a place of guilt or indulgence but from curiosity, you strengthen your internal financial feedback loop. You build fluency. This fluency reduces anxiety—not because you always have overflow, but because when you don't, you understand *why*. You can adjust without panic.

This reframing also helps resist common temptations around irregular windfalls. A consistent pattern of overflow tells you whether your core system is healthy enough to absorb a bonus or windfall without destabilisation. It becomes a baseline health metric. If you're running lean with no overflow and you receive a £4,000 tax refund, that event will likely distort your allocations—because there's no absorptive capacity. But if your system generates regular, modest overflow, the same £4,000 can be spread according to your known proportions or redirected to the buckets currently underfunded. In this way, *overflow becomes a readiness metric—a sign of systemic elasticity.*

It also functions as a calibration mechanism across life stages. When people have children, start businesses, receive promotions, or shift geographies, spending patterns evolve. But these transitions are rarely mapped directly to budget categories in real time. Overflow—when observed with care—tells you where assumptions no longer match behaviour. You may think your Security bucket is underfunded, but if Overflow grows consistently while that bucket remains untouched, the problem may lie in perception, not allocation. Conversely, if Overflow disappears while Growth and Joy are being maxed out, you may be undervaluing your Safety or Essentials categories. This doesn't mean you're spending "wrong." It means your model needs a conversation.

And that's what this is, fundamentally: *a conversation with your money in its most honest form.* Overflow is uncommitted. It has no performance review. It doesn't arrive with expectations. That's what makes it so revealing. You can lie to yourself about your goals, your intentions, your frugality—but you cannot lie to the fact that £320 has landed in Overflow four months in a row. The question is: *Why?* And: *Now what?*

To treat Overflow as an opportunity scanner is to shift from passive budgeting to active financial strategy. It requires periodic review—not obsessive tracking, but structured curiosity. Once a quarter, look at the pattern. Has overflow appeared? Increased? Decreased? Vanished? Is it consistent with your expectations? Does it reflect a change in behaviour, income, or costs? Are you using it to reinforce intentional allocations, or is it silently bleeding into lifestyle upgrades you didn't consciously choose?

This level of engagement doesn't make you rigid. It makes you responsive. It turns excess into signal, signal into insight, and insight into evolution. And perhaps most importantly, it preserves your buckets as living tools—not static rules. When money arrives that doesn't yet belong anywhere, the point is not to invent a reason to spend it. Nor is it to sequester it indefinitely out of fear. The point is to listen. *Overflow is your budget's way of telling you that something has changed. Your only task is to pay attention—and respond accordingly.*

Because in the end, money is not just a reflection of earning or spending. It's a reflection of noticing. And overflow is where the noticing begins.

Chapter 8
Rewiring Money Habits

Most people don't stumble with money due to a lack of knowledge. They falter because knowledge alone rarely alters behaviour. Awareness is necessary, yes, but it is not sufficient. Cognitive insight does not automatically override entrenched routines, nor does it inoculate against the pull of convenience, impulse, or exhaustion. In practice, even those armed with detailed spreadsheets, access to financial education, and strong motivation find themselves slipping—overspending here, deferring savings there, drifting from what they intellectually "know" they should do. The error isn't ignorance. The error is overestimating the power of will in a system designed against sustained behavioural change.

If your financial system requires near-constant vigilance to function, it is brittle by design. Behavioural inertia is the human default. Systems that endure are those that reduce friction, automate follow-through, and harmonise with existing habits—not those demanding heroic, ongoing effort. This chapter begins with a central premise: the success of any budgeting system, including the five-bucket model, hinges less on understanding and more on embedding it into your environment, routines, and mental defaults.

Psychology makes this point unequivocal. Motivation is fleeting; environment is persistent. If you seek financial consistency—saving regularly, spending consciously, allocating with purpose—you are not simply training willpower. You are engineering context. And this is not metaphorical. In a widely cited study, participants who placed gym clothes beside their bed were significantly more likely to exercise the following morning. Behaviour didn't change because motivation surged; it changed because the first step was made easier. Money behaves the same way.

Want to review your budget weekly? Don't merely schedule a reminder. Anchor it to an existing routine—Sunday coffee, your train commute, the ritual of closing the week's tasks. Behavioural scientists call this habit stacking: linking a new behaviour to a pre-existing one so the anchor stabilises the new habit. In financial life, this might mean pairing your payday notification with a five-minute check of bucket allocations, or syncing your Joy spending review with your calendar check for social plans. The goal is not creating rituals in isolation; it is leveraging what already holds.

This reframes discipline. Conventional wisdom assumes meaningful financial change demands painful cuts, iron will, or dramatic resets. That's the glamourised fantasy of transformation, not the reality. Sustainable change is subtle. It feels almost frictionless. A small tweak to your banking app to display bucket balances. A recurring payday transfer pre-allocating overflow. A gentle notification nudging reflection after a non-essential purchase. These "tiny wins" compound over time, reinforcing identity: someone who acts with intention around money. Breakthrough lies in consistency, not magnitude.

A pernicious myth in personal finance is that small shifts are meaningless. Neuroscience suggests otherwise. Dopamine—the neurotransmitter tied to motivation and reward—spikes not only on goal completion, but with progress itself. Measurable progress does not demand grand gestures; it requires feedback loops. This is why the five-bucket system excels: it externalises intention. Goals are no longer vague: "save more" becomes tangible. Growth or Security can be monitored. Joy can be honoured or observed as neglected.

Take Rajiv, a junior doctor in Bristol. Erratic hospital shifts and student loans made routine financial habits elusive. Traditional budgeting tools felt rigid, misaligned with his unpredictable schedule. By linking financial reviews to his shift handover—checking his five buckets during post-call meals—he gradually made the practice natural, even comforting. Within three months, automated allocations were set up, impulsive spending reduced, and a micro-budget for Joy established. None of these actions were dramatic, but they cultivated agency and rhythm amidst chaos.

Timing matters. "How long until it feels automatic?" is a common question. The truth: longer than you think, shorter than you fear. Research suggests an average habit takes 66 days to embed, though the range spans 18 to 254 days, depending on complexity, context, and consistency. The focus should be checkpoints: at two weeks, is it easier than when you began? At six weeks, are friction points fewer? At three months, do routines survive stress or distraction? Progress is marked by permanence, not perfection.

Permanence does not equate to rigidity. You may miss a week, err, or feel resistance—and still return without shame. This is the distinction between systems that support and systems that punish. Many abandon budgeting the moment deviation occurs, believing the structure broken. Well-designed systems accommodate deviation, adapting without collapse. The five-bucket model encourages this: periodic rebalancing, overflow scanning, recalibration—not fixed targets that punish life's fluidity.

Philosophically, rewiring financial habits acknowledges that humans are not purely rational. We are creatures of pattern, energy, stress, social influence, fatigue, and evolving identity. Expecting logic alone to govern finances is naïve, even cruel. Effective systems respect psychology—they account for bad days, forgotten transfers, occasional indulgences—and gently return us to centre.

This chapter is neither pep talk nor tactical checklist. It is a guide to designing a financial ecosystem where good behaviours are easier, defaults wiser, effort sparing but effective. It aligns habits with values without demanding transformation into someone else.

Real change does not come from momentary better choices; it comes from structuring moments so that better choices occur naturally. Rewiring is quiet: subtle reshaping of the everyday, embedding intention rather than imposing discipline.

Behaviour evolves not through force, but fluency. Not overnight, but gradually. One habit at a time, one choice at a time, until new behaviour is no longer a struggle—or even a strategy—it is simply who you are.

Why Awareness Isn't Enough

Knowing what to do and doing it consistently are rarely the same thing. The gap between financial awareness and financial action is not a matter of intelligence, motivation, or even values. It is behavioural inertia—the stubborn persistence of existing routines, regardless of their alignment with our goals. Most budgeting frameworks presume that once a person understands the problem, they will naturally change. But the science of behaviour tells a different story: *awareness is only the starting point*. Left unsupported by system design, even the most financially literate individual will revert to defaults when under stress, distracted, or fatigued.

Behavioural economists have shown that people routinely make decisions that contradict their long-term self-interest, not because they lack information but because of how their environment cues behaviour. In a now-classic study on organ donation, the only significant difference in participation rates across countries was whether the system was opt-in or opt-out. The default choice—not personal belief—determined whether people took action. Apply this insight to financial habits, and the implications are clear: *if good money behaviour is optional or effortful, most people won't follow through consistently*.

Consider automatic retirement contributions. In workplaces where employees are auto-enrolled into pension plans, participation rates skyrocket. Where opt-in is required, participation drops—even among employees who say they intend to sign up. This isn't a failure of values. It's a failure of friction. *Friction is the enemy of follow-through*. And in the context of personal finance, friction hides in dozens of small places: needing to open a separate app to check your savings, remembering to transfer money after a bill is paid, manually moving overflow funds every month. Each step adds a cognitive cost, and over time, those costs compound until the behaviour collapses.

This is why *design matters more than discipline*. Systems that eliminate unnecessary choice points, automate recurring behaviours, and visually reinforce progress are more effective than those that rely on motivation or self-control. One practical implication for anyone using the five-bucket model is to engineer the environment so that the right decisions happen without the need for frequent deliberation. For example, splitting direct deposits into separate accounts mapped to the buckets ensures allocation happens before spending decisions ever arise. Linking the Joy bucket to a specific card or wallet app gives visual feedback on whether you're honouring your values—or drifting.

Automation is not about abdicating responsibility. It is about *freeing cognitive bandwidth* to focus on more meaningful decisions. When basic financial behaviours—saving, allocating, reviewing—are systematised, we reduce the risk of decision fatigue and increase the probability of sustained success. But automation alone is not enough. It must be paired with intentional design—one that respects behavioural realities rather than idealised models of rationality. This includes rethinking physical, digital, and social cues that shape financial behaviour. Where does your budgeting app live on your home screen? How often do your financial goals surface visually in your day-to-day life? Are your key decisions embedded into existing routines or isolated as tasks to "get around to"?

Take the case of Lena, a freelance designer in Manchester. Despite a deep knowledge of personal finance, she found herself chronically under-saving. Budgeting tools made her feel temporarily in control, but her habits never stuck. After reflecting on her daily environment, she redesigned her system. She set her bank's homepage to display progress bars for each of her five buckets. She automated transfers by percentage rather than fixed amounts, so they adjusted to fluctuating income. She moved her Joy and Growth funds to separate digital wallets to reduce impulsive blending. Within months, her savings rate increased—not because she tried harder, but because *she designed less opportunity to fail.*

Another underestimated tool in habit maintenance is *reducing the number of decisions altogether*. Every choice we make requires a small dose of energy. Even beneficial ones. When financial behaviours are too reliant on choice—whether to spend, save, allocate, or rebalance—they become vulnerable to the mental noise of everyday life. But when defaults are engineered intelligently, the behaviour becomes nearly automatic. This is the underlying psychology of choice architecture—a principle pioneered by Thaler and Sunstein in their work on "nudge" theory. They found that people often stick with the default option, not because it's best, but because it's easiest. The same applies to recurring money decisions. *Ease beats intention.*

This insight is particularly important for people who identify as disciplined or organised. Ironically, those who pride themselves on their ability to manage complexity often resist automation because they trust their willpower. But over time, complexity wears down even the most disciplined minds. The real skill isn't managing friction. It's eliminating it. The better your system, the fewer heroic decisions you'll need to make.

It's worth pausing here to distinguish automation from abdication. Delegating behaviours to systems does not mean disengaging from financial life. On the contrary, well-designed automation *increases engagement by reducing anxiety*. When you trust that essential actions are happening in the background—savings being swept, bills being buffered, buckets being funded—you have more mental space to reflect, review, and plan. You can engage with your financial life from a place of calm rather than crisis.

But even the best systems require periodic recalibration. One danger of full automation is drift—when habits continue unchecked even as circumstances change. This is why *environmental feedback loops* matter. Are you seeing weekly indicators of how your money is flowing across the buckets? Are you setting time aside monthly or quarterly to re-align your rules with your goals? These are not passive reviews. They are rituals of intentionality. And without them, even a well-designed system can become misaligned.

Behavioural change also benefits from *visual accountability*. Seeing progress matters. Just as fitness apps use rings, streaks, or milestones to trigger motivation, financial systems should surface progress in a way that's tangible and affirming. This could be a dashboard that shows the percentage of your Growth bucket funded relative to your annual goal. Or a weekly email that summarises how you spent Joy funds, prompting you to reflect on whether that spending felt aligned with your values. These are not gimmicks—they're behavioural scaffolds. *They reinforce identity by making invisible wins visible.*

It's important to recognise that behavioural design is not one-size-fits-all. What works for someone with a salaried job and predictable expenses may not work for someone with variable income or caregiving duties. The principle, however, remains: *the more behaviour is embedded in your context, the less effort is required to maintain it*. That's why effective design begins with self-awareness. What are your friction points? When does your attention peak and crash? What are the moments of highest vulnerability—late nights, low moods, unexpected expenses—and how can your system absorb those without breaking?

Ultimately, the real shift is in seeing financial systems not as tools you operate, but as environments you inhabit. Environments that support your intentions even when you are distracted, tired, or uncertain. This is the difference between awareness and execution. One tells you what to do. The other ensures it gets done.

Awareness is admirable. Reflection is necessary. But in the messy reality of daily life, *only behaviour changes outcomes.*

And behaviour changes when the environment makes the right action easy, obvious, and consistent. Until that happens, no amount of knowledge will be enough.

Habit Stacking With Buckets

Most people fail at financial behaviour not because of ignorance or apathy, but because their good intentions live in isolation. They exist as separate, fragile resolutions—"I should start reviewing my spending weekly" or "Next month I'll move my overflow to savings"—that require conscious activation every time. Behavioural science has a term for this problem: *decision fatigue*. And the antidote is structure. When behaviours are designed to occur automatically, triggered by events that already happen in daily life, follow-through no longer depends on willpower. This is where *habit stacking* becomes powerful—*a strategic approach to embedding financial habits inside the routines you already do, reliably and without friction.*

The science of habit stacking is rooted in the work of behavioural theorists like BJ Fogg and Charles Duhigg, but it was James Clear who gave it wide traction. The principle is deceptively simple: rather than attempting to build a new routine from scratch, you anchor it to something you already do consistently. "After I brew my morning coffee, I will review my calendar." "When I close my laptop on Friday, I'll review my spending." The existing habit becomes a trigger—automatic, stable, and already woven into your life. The question for our purposes is this: *how can we use these triggers to reinforce the Five-Bucket Budget model so that it becomes not just conceptual, but habitual*?

Start with one of the most predictable patterns in adult life: payday. Salaried or freelance, monthly or fortnightly, income is among the few financial rhythms that arrive with consistency. This makes it an ideal anchor for your core budgeting behaviours. For example, you might create a payday ritual: a ten-minute review of your digital bucket allocations, a glance at your Overflow status, and a brief check-in on any anomalies—unexpected expenses, new subscriptions, or pending renewals. Over time, this ritual becomes reflexive. The arrival of money triggers behaviour, not speculation.

For many people, the most emotionally loaded bucket is Joy. It's also the one most prone to sabotage through guilt, drift, or impulsivity. Which is why tying it to a weekly habit—a Sunday evening review, say—can restore intentionality. Set aside ten minutes to audit Joy spending: did those purchases reflect your values, or were they driven by fatigue, boredom, or comparison? Did your use of Joy money contribute to actual wellbeing or leave a trail of minor regret? This is not a moral inquisition; it is a behavioural checkpoint. *And like all effective habits, it must occur in the same time and place each week to become embedded.*

The strongest financial systems do not rely on giant leaps. They rely on tiny, reliable pulses of action. Behavioural science repeatedly confirms that *frequency beats intensity*. A ten-minute weekly ritual has more staying power than a two-hour monthly overhaul. Why? Because it integrates with life. It respects the bandwidth of real people—working professionals, exhausted parents, students with deadline fatigue. These people do not need more effort. They need more *design*.

Consider an example: Ravi, a civil servant in Birmingham, began habit-stacking his Five-Bucket system during his commute. Every Monday, while on the train, he reviewed a pre-set snapshot of his buckets in his budgeting app. This triggered a three-minute reflection: Does this week require adjusting any allocations? Is any bucket dangerously low or swelling with unused funds? Once a month, that same Monday commute included a note to self: scan for upcoming costs (e.g. council tax, holidays, or gift expenses) and shift funds if needed. Because this ritual was anchored to a habitual activity—the train ride—it persisted long after the initial motivation faded.

Anchoring also works for low-energy routines. For instance, if you already check your email first thing in the morning, consider adding a glance at your high-level budget dashboard before replying to messages. Not a deep dive—just enough to remind yourself of current allocations, recent spending, or upcoming bills. This micro-exposure builds *financial fluency through repetition*, much like checking the weather builds intuition about seasonal changes.

To ensure habit stacking succeeds in the long term, it must obey a core behavioural principle: *low friction, high reward*. The habit must be easy to do and emotionally reinforcing. If your bucket check-in feels like a chore, you will unconsciously avoid it. But if it gives you a sense of control, momentum, or relief, it will begin to reinforce itself. This is where emotional design plays a critical role. Pair your financial review with a pleasure—your favourite tea, a quiet room, a moment of peace. This pairing transforms the habit from task to ritual. And rituals last.

One barrier to habit stacking in financial life is what psychologists call the *intention-behaviour gap*. People know what they want to do, and even why, but they don't translate that into regular action. One reason is that the trigger is too vague. "I'll check my budget later" has no anchor. But "After my weekly grocery run, I'll update my Essential bucket" has specificity. The best financial habits are *time- and context-bound*. They live in a particular moment, not in the abstract.

There is also a deeper behavioural truth worth naming: *consistency changes identity*. When you act in a financially aligned way, over and over, even in tiny increments, you begin to internalise the identity of someone who is financially competent, intentional, and self-directed. This identity shift is not motivational fluff. It is foundational. Research on habit formation shows that the most durable behaviours are those aligned with a person's sense of self. If you see yourself as "bad with money," you will unconsciously resist behaviours that contradict that belief. But if your system gives you frequent, visible evidence that you are acting like someone who is on top of their finances, your identity shifts. And behaviour becomes self-reinforcing.

Habit stacking also provides a subtle but powerful benefit: *it reduces cognitive switching costs.* By pairing financial behaviours with routines that already exist, you avoid the mental overhead of deciding when to do them. You don't need to set aside new time slots, negotiate motivation, or wait for inspiration. The system runs on what is already there. This is especially crucial for people managing complex lives—entrepreneurs with unpredictable schedules, carers with erratic demands, or students juggling shifting deadlines. For these people, elegant simplicity matters more than ambitious planning.

It's important to acknowledge that habit stacking works best when the feedback loop is tight. The more immediate the signal of success, the stronger the reinforcement. For financial behaviours, that might mean visually seeing your Joy bucket shrink after a purchase—or grow after a week of restraint. It might mean receiving a weekly email summary that quantifies your bucket movements and highlights areas of stability or concern. These signals are not ornamental. *They create behavioural closure.* And closure fuels continuation.

One of the most underutilised opportunities for habit stacking lies in shared routines. Couples, flatmates, or families can build collective rituals around financial check-ins. Not elaborate budgeting meetings, but five-minute weekly syncs: "Here's where our Joy bucket stands. Do we want to spend it this weekend or save it for a bigger moment?" These micro-conversations, when habitualised, de-escalate financial tension and embed shared clarity.

Of course, habit stacking is not magic. It does not eliminate the need for larger strategic thinking. But it *makes strategy stick*. You can set brilliant budget allocations, but if you never return to them, they erode. You can design a perfect bucket structure, but if the system doesn't get used, it decays. Habit stacking turns theory into practice. Repeated, lived, integrated practice.

The goal of the Five-Bucket Budget is not just awareness. It is embodiment. And embodiment happens not through Herculean effort, but through frictionless repetition. Every time you check your buckets before ordering takeaway, reallocate overflow on a Friday afternoon, or pause to reflect on your Joy spending while sipping tea, you are reinforcing a system that serves you. The more tightly those behaviours are tied to your real life, the less likely they are to drift into forgettable aspiration.

Ultimately, *habit stacking is not about doing more*. It is about making what matters inevitable.

Tiny Wins, Not Big Sacrifices

The most persistent myth in personal finance is the belief that transformation requires radical upheaval—cutting out every luxury, cancelling every subscription, and overhauling one's life in a single sweeping gesture. This thinking is not only demoralising; it's demonstrably false.

Behavioural science, cognitive psychology, and lived human experience all point to a more durable truth: *change that lasts is rarely dramatic—it is incremental, consistent, and nearly invisible while it's happening*. In the context of the Five-Bucket Budget, anchoring success does not hinge on heroic sacrifice but on modest, repeatable actions. What builds financial confidence and control isn't austerity; it's the *compounding power of tiny wins*.

Tiny wins work because they sidestep the emotional resistance that big sacrifices inevitably trigger. Humans are wired to avoid pain, including the psychological discomfort of perceived loss. When a budgeting system demands drastic cuts or immediate self-denial, the internal cost often outweighs the perceived benefit. This is why cold-turkey savings plans collapse and why elaborate spreadsheets gather dust after a few weeks. Big, abstract goals like "get out of debt" or "save for retirement" lack frictionless entry points. But small wins—declining a delivery meal and moving £15 to your Freedom bucket instead—feel doable. They require little activation energy, and they produce immediate, measurable momentum.

Momentum matters more than magnitude. One client—a 29-year-old nurse earning just above the national average—built a consistent practice of shifting just £5 into her Wealth bucket every time she walked instead of taking an Uber. Over time, this tiny act became automatic. In 14 months, without ever "sacrificing," she had over £800 saved—enough to cover her dental work without debt. What matters here isn't the amount. It's the *identity reinforcement*. She became someone who noticed small opportunities and acted on them. *Each win wasn't just a deposit—it was a message to herself: I am paying attention. I have agency.*

Small, deliberate behaviours build habits. And habits build systems. Take the Joy bucket, often viewed as indulgent or optional. Many readers begin their budgeting journey by restricting Joy spending entirely, believing this sacrifice demonstrates seriousness. But this approach is psychologically unsustainable. What works better is a micro-upgrade strategy: spend £10 on a solo cinema ticket instead of £60 on a rushed dinner out. Choose an experience that *truly delights*, not one that signals status. Log the feeling afterward—was it worth it? Would you do it again? In doing so, you teach yourself not just how to spend less, but how to spend *well*. The habit of reflection is itself a win.

Critically, the power of tiny wins lies in their capacity to *accumulate without triggering fatigue*. Big sacrifices drain willpower. But a system that cues small adjustments—rounding up card payments to nudge savings, pre-allocating £25 weekly for guilt-free Joy, or auditing recurring subscriptions quarterly—feels light. Because it is. Yet the results, over months and years, are profound. It is this *non-disruptive persistence* that gives the Five-Bucket model its unique potency.

There's also a neurochemical reason tiny wins work: they deliver hits of dopamine, the brain's motivation chemical. Not in the artificial way that a social media notification does, but in the deeper, self-generated sense of progress. When you act in alignment with your goals—no matter how small the gesture—your brain rewards you. This reward loop is crucial to habit formation. It explains why ticking a task off a list feels satisfying, and why people who track behaviours (however modest) are more likely to maintain them. Financial behaviour is no different. Whether you note a £3 win or a £300 transfer, the psychological signature is the same: I did something that mattered.

Importantly, tiny wins protect against the self-sabotaging logic of all-or-nothing thinking. One of the most corrosive beliefs in personal finance is "I've already failed this month, so it doesn't matter what I do now." This belief collapses the entire budget into a pass/fail binary. But if your framework celebrates small wins—even amid setbacks—you maintain momentum. Overspent on takeaways? Don't spiral. Instead, take five minutes to rebalance your buckets or cancel an unused subscription. A small corrective action *restores narrative control*. You are no longer failing. You are adapting.

The Five-Bucket model thrives on this mindset. Because it doesn't impose perfection, it encourages iteration. Overflow this month? Use it as feedback, not as judgement. Did your Freedom bucket feel too tight? Note it, adjust. Each decision becomes a low-stakes opportunity to experiment and learn. And learning—small, embodied, emotionally neutral learning—is the foundation of long-term financial confidence.

Case studies reveal this truth across income levels. Maria, a single mother on Universal Credit, used her weekly grocery trip as a budgeting checkpoint. She added one reflective question: "Is there a non-essential I can skip this week and redirect to my Safety bucket?" Often the answer was a £2 snack or extra coffee. But over 10 months, that habit funded a £500 emergency cushion—her first in years. Not because she earned more. Not because she sacrificed. *Because she repeated a tiny decision that respected her reality.*

Contrast that with Raj, a high-earning consultant who attempted a top-down overhaul—zeroing out discretionary spending, overfunding savings, and trying to micromanage every bucket. He lasted six weeks. The system felt brittle and punitive. He then rebuilt using tiny interventions: a Friday Joy audit, automatic transfers to Wealth, and a simple rule—he could only reallocate Overflow once a month, forcing reflection. The result wasn't just sustainability; it was a sense of control that *didn't require white-knuckle discipline*.

Another benefit of this approach is that it builds *psychological safety*. When people feel they must be perfect with money, they become avoidant. Small wins, on the other hand, create permission to engage. This is especially important for those recovering from financial shame—whether due to past debt, family dynamics, or cultural scripts. In these contexts, tiny wins function as *repair mechanisms*, gradually building a new relationship with money that feels competent, not critical.

Crucially, these wins must be visible. Without tracking—even in the simplest way—they lose their power. Visibility can be as minimal as a weekly note in your phone, a physical jar for Joy cash, or a dashboard that colour-codes your buckets. The goal is not obsessive measurement. It's affirmation. You want to see your system working. You want evidence that your choices matter. And when you do, you'll make more of them.

This principle also applies to financial literacy. Trying to "master" investing, tax codes, or mortgage structures in a single weekend is overwhelming. But reading one article per week, setting a calendar reminder to update your savings goals monthly, or having one money conversation per month—that's a stack of tiny wins that becomes *financial competence by osmosis*. You are not passively absorbing information. You are practising orientation. And orientation is what allows learning to stick.

What makes the Five-Bucket model particularly suited to this philosophy is that it provides built-in feedback loops. When you spend, you deplete a bucket. When you underspend, you create Overflow. When you have a windfall, you rebalance. Each of these is an opportunity to act—*not react*. The system is not static; it's interactive. And every interaction, no matter how small, is a chance to practice. *And practice—not purity—is the hallmark of financial maturity*.

To move from theory to embodiment, consider adopting what behavioural economists call "commitment devices."

Not harsh constraints, but small nudges that increase follow-through. Set a Joy cap each week and challenge yourself to come in under budget. Let any unspent Joy roll into Freedom. Use a visual tracker. Share a goal with a trusted friend. Gamify your budget, if that's your style. The specific method matters less than the principle: *you are stacking intentional repetitions that reinforce identity*. That is the work.

And that work adds up. Quietly, without drama, these wins begin to accumulate. £5 here. A paused subscription there. A conversation you used to avoid. A moment of restraint. A choice made in line with your buckets instead of against them. At first, these seem minor. Forgettable. But eventually, the system reveals its shape. You are not merely "budgeting." You are participating in *a designed, evolving, values-based relationship with your money*. And the gateway to that relationship is not suffering. It is the next tiny win.

How Long Until It Feels Natural?

Ask anyone who has tried to adopt a new financial system, from zero-based budgeting to envelope methods, and you'll likely hear a variation of the same refrain: *"It felt awkward at first."* This is not a flaw of the system—it's a feature of being human. When we introduce new cognitive routines, particularly those that challenge long-held beliefs or behaviours, friction is inevitable. The mistake most people make is misinterpreting this discomfort as failure rather than *proof of growth*. So the more relevant question isn't "Will this feel strange?" but *"How long until it doesn't?"*

To answer that with precision, we need to dismantle the myth of instant adaptation. Most behaviour change literature references the now-ubiquitous "21 days to form a habit" mantra—a figure originating from Dr. Maxwell Maltz's observations in the 1960s. But more rigorous contemporary research from University College London found that, on average, *it takes 66 days for a behaviour to become automatic*, with substantial variance depending on complexity, environment, and emotional resistance. Applied to the Five-Bucket Budget model, this means the system doesn't become intuitive simply by understanding it; it becomes natural through *repetition in context*.

Consider what you're actually doing when you implement the Five-Bucket system. You're not just reallocating funds—you're restructuring *attention*. You're tracking spending, reinterpreting joy, questioning defaults, and making deliberate choices about money that most people never consciously examine. This requires not only logistical coordination but *neurological rewiring*. Neural pathways associated with habitual spending—whether mindless Amazon purchases, always choosing takeaway, or avoiding your savings app—don't vanish because you want them to. They weaken when you stop using them and *strengthen when you reinforce the new ones*. The transition period between those two states is often cognitively taxing.

This is why setting realistic expectations matters. If after four weeks the buckets still feel clunky, or you forget to update your log, or you second-guess a Joy allocation, that's not regression—it's *data*. And that data is useful. It points to where friction still lives: perhaps your environment isn't reinforcing the habit, or your system isn't visible enough, or your rules are too vague. This stage—let's call it the "conscious recalibration phase"—typically lasts 4 to 8 weeks. During this window, the system still feels like something you're *doing,* not something you *are*. That distinction matters.

Checkpoint systems are invaluable here—not just for accountability, but for psychological reinforcement. Consider using three benchmark moments in your first 90 days:

1. **Week 4: Awareness without automation.** At this point, you should have basic familiarity with each bucket. You can roughly predict your allocations, but it still takes effort. Mistakes are common. The goal isn't perfection; it's to track without avoidance. Are you logging activity weekly? Do you know where your overflow is going? If yes, you're further along than you think.

2. **Week 8: Increased fluency with mild inconsistency.** By now, some habits are stabilising. You may have repeated your paycheck ritual four times. You've likely adjusted allocations after misjudging. The core question is: *Do you feel more confident?* Not infallible—just more in control than you did before. If so, you're transitioning from deliberate practice to intuitive preference.

3. **Week 12: Baseline normalisation.** This is when the Five-Bucket framework should begin to feel like the "default operating system." It doesn't mean you never err. But errors are now signals, not threats. You're less reactive, more reflective. This is the point at which you've likely built enough momentum for the system to sustain itself with minimal cognitive effort. You no longer ask "What should I do?" You ask "What does my system tell me to do?"

It's worth noting that "natural" doesn't mean effortless. Even the most seasoned professionals—planners, analysts, or wealth coaches—encounter friction when personal circumstances shift. Natural means *familiar and meaningful.* It means the system has emotional resonance. You see Joy spending as an act of design, not guilt. You view Overflow as a signal, not a fluke. You trust your own decisions because they're grounded in pattern, not panic.

To accelerate this normalisation, environment matters. Behavioural design teaches us that habits are easier to form when *cues are obvious and friction is low*. If you have to hunt for your spreadsheet, you won't update it. If your app is buried on your phone, you'll forget to transfer. But if the Five-Bucket dashboard lives on your home screen, or if your Joy spending is tracked in a visible calendar, your system starts working *with* your brain, not against it. Redesigning your environment isn't about gimmicks; it's about aligning intention with access.

Automation helps too—not because it replaces discipline, but because it frees cognitive bandwidth. Set a recurring calendar nudge to review your buckets. Automate transfers into Wealth or Safety after payday. Use round-up savings tools or spending alerts. These aren't crutches; they are *architecture.* They scaffold the new identity you're building: someone who stewards their money with clarity and calm.

But alongside design and automation, *emotional pacing* is essential. Many people unconsciously expect a motivational high to carry them through the first phase of change. When that high dips—often in Week 3 or 4—they misinterpret fatigue as incompatibility. That's the danger zone. If you push through—especially by leaning on *rituals* rather than mood—you'll pass the inflection point. One client reported that the act of making tea before her Saturday budget check-in created a sense of ceremony, making the task feel less like homework and more like stewardship. This tiny emotional anchor helped turn repetition into routine.

Adaptation isn't linear, though. There are regressions. There are weeks where you forget, months where buckets blur, and times when life interrupts your system entirely. That's not failure. *That's reality.* The difference between people who stick with the Five-Bucket model and those who abandon it isn't consistency in action—it's consistency in return. The best users are not the most disciplined. They are the most forgiving. When you miss a month, you reboot. When you overspend in one bucket, you rebalance. When a windfall arrives, you consult the model rather than improvising. These recovery reflexes *are the system.*

Critically, adaptation time also depends on *psychological starting point*. If your past financial habits were chaotic or emotionally fraught, your learning curve will include not just mechanics but trust-building. Trust in yourself. Trust in a structure. Trust in delayed gratification. That process takes longer, and it should. You are not just implementing a budget; you are constructing a new relationship with a part of life you may have ignored, feared, or resented. That emotional layering must be acknowledged—not pathologised.

It's also why progress is best tracked qualitatively, not just quantitatively. Yes, the numbers matter. But so do your thoughts and feelings. Keep a brief log after each bucket review: *What felt easy? What felt strained? What surprised me?* These reflections provide insight into where your habits are sticking—and where they need reinforcement. In six months, these entries will become a map of your transformation.

Ultimately, the question "How long until it feels natural?" isn't about time. It's about *exposure with reflection*. How often are you engaging with the model? Are you noticing the feedback it provides? Are you adjusting with intention, or defaulting to old scripts? The Five-Bucket Budget is not a compliance tool. It's an *attention framework*. And what feels natural, in any domain, is what we've chosen to attend to consistently.

So if you're still waiting for budgeting to feel seamless, stop waiting and start *practising*. That is where the shift begins.

Not in the calendar, but in the decision you make next. Whether it's a single transfer, a 10-minute review, or one clear reallocation—you are rehearsing the future. And one day, likely sooner than you expect, you'll realise that what once felt foreign now feels like fluency. You'll notice that the buckets no longer require effort to recall. They will have become the backdrop of your choices, the architecture of your agency, the quiet rhythm beneath your financial life. And it will feel—finally, and fully—natural.

Chapter 9
Adapting the System to Real Life

No financial system, however elegantly conceived, survives contact with reality unchanged. Budgets in theory are tidy exercises; budgets in life are messy, relational, and stubbornly human. They collide with competing priorities, emotional baggage, logistical chaos, and the unpredictable rhythms of daily existence. The true test of any model isn't its performance under ideal conditions, but how gracefully it flexes under real ones: shared lives, fluctuating incomes, dependent care, and the asymmetries of modern responsibility. The Five-Bucket Budget was never meant to be fragile; it was designed as scaffolding—durable, capable of bending without breaking.

This chapter addresses a truth too often overlooked in personal finance: money decisions rarely exist in isolation. They are embedded in relationships, roles, and obligations. A newly married couple merges not just bank accounts, but financial expectations shaped by different upbringings. A freelancer may thrive for three months and panic in the fourth. A caregiver balancing children and ageing parents navigates a financial tightrope that demands more than motivational slogans—it requires structural empathy. The principle is simple, though often resisted: complex circumstances demand systems that are both rigorous and forgiving. Simplicity must not mean rigidity; clarity must not become constraint.

Consider partnerships. For couples, the question is seldom whether to combine finances, but how to do so in a manner that honours autonomy while fostering accountability.

Traditional models push extremes—full merger or strict independence. Both often fail under stress. The Five-Bucket framework offers a third way: modularity. Rather than quibbling over who spent on dinner or whose turn it is to cover the car repair, couples can align around buckets instead of micro-behaviours. Money conversations shift from audits to agreements. Agreeing on a "Joy" bucket, for instance, allows each partner to spend freely within that allocation—without surveillance, suspicion, or passive-aggressive accounting. The focus moves from control to coordination, acknowledging that trust is strengthened not by eliminating risk, but by agreeing on rules of engagement.

Parenting illustrates another dimension. Teaching children about money has often meant allowances or chore payments devoid of context. Integrating the Five-Bucket logic, however, teaches a deeper lesson: money as philosophy, not merely medium. When a child allocates part of pocket money to "Wealth," "Joy," or "Giving," they internalise a framework for values-driven decision-making. Transactions become reflections of intention. One family, using colour-coded jars representing the buckets, witnessed their eight-year-old purchase a birthday gift from the "Giving" jar. More than a transaction, it was an act of agency—laying the groundwork for lifelong financial confidence.

Flexibility becomes crucial when income resists regularity. Freelancers, seasonal workers, and artists find traditional monthly targets misleading at best. With variable income, stability must be manufactured. The Five-Bucket model shifts the unit of budgeting from calendar months to allocation logic. Each payment becomes a recalibration: "Where should this money go across all five buckets?" Lean months demand thoughtful prioritisation; abundant months invite repair of neglected buckets or preloading future obligations. This responsive approach mirrors successful businesses: they do not predict every contingency with spreadsheets, they adjust allocations in real time with an eye toward sustainability.

The sandwich generation—caring simultaneously for children and ageing parents—presents yet another scenario. Their financial landscape is triage in motion. They manage personal goals while absorbing others' histories and shaping futures. Here, the Five-Bucket model becomes a relational map, articulating trade-offs with clarity: "This month's medical expense comes from Safety, which means Joy or Wealth must adjust next month." Transparency, even when uncomfortable, grants permission to prioritise without guilt. One caregiver remarked that naming the buckets reduced decision fatigue: choices that once felt like constant sacrifice became visible and shared.

Across couples, parents, freelancers, and caregivers, a pattern emerges. Success is not perfect adherence; it is the ability to use the buckets as a language for complexity. Life will stretch any system. The Five-Bucket model does not resist that stretch—it provides orientation. It anchors decisions in shared principles, diagnoses friction, highlights imbalance, and names trade-offs. This is the difference between reacting to money and leading it.

Adaptation does not dilute the philosophy; it strengthens it. Systems that cannot flex under complexity are not intelligent. The Five-Bucket framework remains structurally sound across contexts: a retiree downsizing and a twenty-year-old saving their first emergency fund can both use it effectively. It works in abundance and scarcity alike. The logic is constant; the application is fluid.

Financial models, when aligned with life, become identity infrastructure. Buckets reflect more than spending—they mirror evolving values. Over time, they reveal patterns: leaning too heavily into Security at the expense of Joy, giving consistently without replenishing Wealth, outsourcing clarity to a partner instead of co-owning the vision. These are existential, not technical, questions. The Five-Bucket framework, used honestly, offers a compass, not a rulebook. The goal is not perfection, but orientation—anchored clarity amid shifting circumstances.

This chapter is about making the system yours. Joint finances, teaching a child to respect a fiver, smoothing variable income, or navigating care for multiple generations—your context is valid. Complexity is not a barrier to financial intelligence; it is why intelligence matters. The Five-Bucket model accommodates that truth. Now, the task is to live it—not as theory, but through the details of real life.

For Couples: Aligning Shared Buckets

Money is rarely just about numbers when two people share a life. In practice, it's a proxy for priorities, habits, boundaries, and often unspoken fears. When couples attempt to align financially without a shared system, discussions about spending can quickly devolve into power struggles or emotional avoidance. It's not that most people are irresponsible or irrational—it's that they often lack *a common structure* to interpret decisions. What the Five-

Bucket framework provides is not just a way to allocate money; it's a way to translate values into shared action, so that both partners can co-own their financial story *without micromanaging each other's decisions*. The goal isn't uniformity—it's clarity, autonomy, and mutual respect embedded within a cohesive plan.

One of the most pervasive myths in joint financial planning is that unity means full merging—same accounts, same decisions, same approach to every penny. This assumption is not only unnecessary but often counterproductive. The idea that a couple must agree on *everything* before they can move forward financially is a recipe for delay and resentment. The Five-Bucket model sidesteps this trap by building collaboration around purpose-defined containers. Rather than trying to control one another's behaviour line by line, couples agree on the flow of funds into *buckets*—Safety, Wealth, Essentials, Joy, and Overflow. Each bucket has its own logic, its own intended function. That clarity gives both structure and freedom. When money is pre-allocated by mutual agreement, individuals retain discretion within boundaries, and conversations become strategic rather than reactive.

Take, for instance, the Joy bucket. Without a structure, one partner's spontaneous weekend trip can feel to the other like an unapproved withdrawal from shared goals. But if both have agreed that 5–10% of net income is earmarked for personal or shared indulgences, the same purchase becomes an expression of agreed-upon value, not a breach of trust.

The difference lies in the *pre-commitment,* not the transaction. Similarly, if the Essentials bucket—covering rent, groceries, utilities, and other baseline obligations—is funded automatically from a joint account, the energy usually spent on micro-tracking each other's spending can be redirected to more productive forms of planning.

This doesn't mean that every couple must pool all their income into shared buckets. The model accommodates multiple configurations: some may prefer to fund joint buckets proportionally to income, while retaining private accounts for discretionary spending. Others may merge completely. What matters is *not* the structure itself but the clarity of shared intention. The bucket system allows for negotiation over *categories* rather than individual purchases. One couple earning significantly different incomes may decide to split contributions to each bucket based on percentage rather than amount, so that each feels equitably invested without enforcing false symmetry. This protects against silent resentments, particularly where one partner earns more and the other manages more unpaid labour—such as childcare or elder care.

Crucially, aligning shared buckets is not a one-off conversation. It's an ongoing calibration process. Life changes—so must allocations. A new baby, a job loss, a relocation, or even a shift in ambition can all warrant adjustments. The discipline of regular check-ins, ideally monthly or quarterly, helps keep the system alive. These aren't budget meetings in the traditional, soul-draining sense. They're strategy sessions. They ask: *Do our buckets still reflect our current priorities?* If not, what needs to shift? Framing the conversation this way encourages mutual reflection rather than defensiveness. It moves the focus from "Who spent what?" to "Are we still building the life we want?"

But even the best-designed system cannot function without shared psychological safety. Money is emotionally loaded, often shaped by childhood scripts, cultural norms, and past traumas. One partner may equate savings with security; another may associate it with hoarding. One may view giving as a moral obligation; the other may see it as impractical. These are not trivial differences. They inform every financial decision at a subconscious level. The Five-Bucket model offers a safe way to surface these tensions because it externalises the decision-making framework. Instead of one person saying, "We need to stop spending on X," the couple can ask, "Does this align with our agreed-upon Joy or Essentials allocation?" That subtle reframe reduces conflict by shifting from personal judgement to shared standards.

An effective entry point for this alignment process is what behavioural economists call a *default intervention*. Rather than asking couples to change everything at once, the model encourages them to build defaults that run automatically unless consciously overridden. For example, auto-transfer rules can move a fixed percentage of income into each bucket the day after payday. Joint tracking dashboards can be configured to show cumulative progress in each category, avoiding the ambiguity that often fuels suspicion. The more that decisions are made once and then executed repeatedly without renegotiation, the less friction accumulates in the day-to-day. This frees up mental bandwidth and builds a sense of partnership-in-motion rather than endless negotiation.

Importantly, transparency does not require surveillance. Not every couple needs to review every purchase together. The point of aligning buckets is to agree in advance on the *boundaries of autonomy*. If one partner has £150 a month from the shared Joy bucket to spend as they wish, no justification should be required unless they exceed it. This principle—freedom within structure—preserves individual dignity while protecting shared goals. It also reduces the likelihood that money will be used as a control mechanism, consciously or not.

Conflict often arises not from overspending, but from mismatched expectations. One partner may believe they're saving aggressively, only to discover the other is quietly redirecting surplus into lifestyle upgrades. In the absence of a visible model like the Five Buckets, these actions are interpreted personally: as betrayal, irresponsibility, or disregard. But when overflow, for instance, is treated as a *signal,* not a surplus—available for discretionary reallocation to Joy, Wealth, or other priorities—partners gain a shared interpretive lens. This fosters strategic dialogue instead of reactive judgment. "We've had more overflow than expected this quarter—should we top up the Wealth bucket or finally take that trip we've talked about?" becomes a constructive question, not a covert tug-of-war.

Shared financial systems are also a form of *emotional intimacy*. They reveal what each person values, what they fear, what trade-offs they're willing to accept. The bucket model can help make these implicit patterns explicit. A couple who always overfunds the Safety bucket but underfunds Joy may discover they're living more defensively than they intend. Conversely, a couple who repeatedly neglects the Wealth bucket may be overly focused on the present at the expense of future security. These are not budgeting failures—they are insights. And when surfaced thoughtfully, they become openings for deeper conversations about life direction, not just money management.

To be clear, no system eliminates tension. There will still be disagreements, moments of friction, and periods of misalignment. But a good system provides a *container* for those tensions—so they don't spill into every other domain of the relationship. With buckets in place, a spending dispute is less likely to metastasise into questions about love, trust, or compatibility. The fight stays where it belongs: in the financial architecture, not in the relationship itself.

Ultimately, aligning shared buckets is not about achieving perfect harmony. It's about designing a system that respects both individuals while enabling a collective vision. It's about shifting from reactive budgeting to proactive decision-making. It's about building a partnership that can navigate complexity without defaulting to micromanagement or silent resentment.

The Five-Bucket system is not a panacea. It's a conversation starter, a container, a tool. But used wisely, it becomes something more: a *shared operating system* for a shared life—one that enables couples not just to manage money, but to design it in service of what matters most to them, together.

For Parents: Teaching Kids With Buckets

There is a profound difference between giving a child money and giving them a framework to understand money. While many well-meaning parents focus on allowances, piggy banks, and sporadic financial lectures, the long-term impact of these tools is often diluted by inconsistency and abstraction. Financial literacy doesn't emerge from isolated moments—it takes root when money management becomes a visible, shared, and habitual part of everyday life. The Five-Bucket Budget offers not merely a tool but a system that can scaffold a child's understanding of value, choice, and consequence in a world increasingly defined by financial complexity.

When financial lessons are introduced too late—often during university or a child's first job—they arrive in the context of debt, anxiety, and urgency. What should have been internalised as habit is instead treated as damage control. By contrast, integrating the Five-Bucket model during childhood allows financial acumen to grow in parallel with a child's maturing judgement. Money becomes demystified not through sermons, but through repetition and active participation.

Begin with visibility. Children cannot emulate what they cannot see. If money is managed silently behind closed doors—digitally automated and emotionally charged—they are left to infer from snippets, moods, or outcomes. But when they see decisions being made across structured categories—Needs, Future, Safety, Joy, and Overflow—they encounter a repeatable, nameable process. This visibility creates vocabulary, and vocabulary makes reflection possible. When a ten-year-old understands that some money is meant for joy now, and some for joy later, they are already engaging in delayed gratification. That's not just financial education—it's cognitive development.

Allowances provide an ideal platform for operationalising the model. A £10 weekly allowance can be split—£4 into Needs (for school supplies or essentials), £2 into Joy (for treats or fun purchases), £2 into Future (for longer-term goals like a game or book), £1 into Safety (a contingency buffer or charity), and £1 into Overflow (to review at month's end). These proportions are not fixed but offer a conceptual structure that mimics adult systems. Over time, children begin to recognise that not all money is meant to be spent immediately, and not all spending brings equal value. Crucially, they learn to *allocate*, not just spend—a behavioural distinction that most adults struggle to master.

Conversation is where values are translated into context. When a child asks, "Why can't I use my Joy money for that toy?" it opens a teaching moment—not for control, but for curiosity. "That's a great idea—what do you think would happen to your Future bucket if you did that every time?" This style of inquiry moves beyond rules into reflection. It also cultivates autonomy by allowing the child to make decisions within a scaffolded system. You're not micromanaging their every purchase; you're equipping them to weigh trade-offs and live with the results.

The role of parental modelling cannot be overstated. If a child observes a parent consistently respecting their own bucket allocations—pausing before dipping into Joy prematurely or discussing how a holiday was funded through consistent savings—they absorb those patterns long before they can articulate them. When a parent says, "That's coming from our Overflow because we did well this month," it doesn't just signal abundance; it signals stewardship. It's a masterclass in value-based decision-making delivered in plain, lived language.

Adolescence presents both a challenge and an opportunity. Teenagers crave autonomy yet often lack financial experience. This is precisely when the framework can be expanded. If a teenager earns income from part-time work, they can manage a personal version of the Five Buckets. They may choose to increase Joy and Future proportions while still contributing to Safety or Overflow. What matters is the continuity of structure—a way to interpret income that is not reactive but proactive. The buckets become not just financial categories, but a mirror of one's values in motion.

Technology can assist, but should not displace intent. Digital banking tools that allow for multiple wallets or sub-accounts can replicate the Five Buckets practically. A child who logs into an app and sees five growing balances—with names that reflect purpose, not vagueness—experiences money as segmented, governed, and trackable. These visual cues reinforce discipline more powerfully than any lecture. The goal is not to gamify saving, but to ground financial behaviour in *design*, not impulse.

Critically, the system is not rigid. Life is fluid, and so is this model. During periods of increased need—such as back-to-school shopping—allocations may shift temporarily. A family might agree to bolster the Needs bucket, drawing temporarily from Joy or Overflow. These recalibrations should not be seen as rule-breaking, but as collaborative budgeting. Children learn not just the rules of allocation, but the *principles of adjustment*. This teaches resilience, not just discipline.

For families managing different levels of income or navigating financial stress, the model remains valid. In fact, it may be more powerful in these contexts. When money is tight, clarity matters more than abundance. Teaching a child that even £5 can be divided meaningfully instils dignity and intentionality. It prevents the all-or-nothing mentality that derails so many adult budgets. You don't need wealth to build wisdom.

Lastly, remember that financial education is not a curriculum but a culture. It isn't delivered in one weekend or even one year. It is embedded in how families talk, decide, and reflect together over time. The Five-Bucket system offers a shared grammar—a way to interpret choices across generations. Parents who use the buckets with consistency and openness will find that they're not just managing their own finances more clearly—they're raising financially literate, reflective children who understand money not as a source of stress or status, but as a tool for thoughtful living.

For Entrepreneurs and Freelancers: Navigating Irregular Income Through the Five-Bucket Model

Predictability is a luxury that most entrepreneurs and freelancers cannot afford. Unlike salaried workers, those with self-directed careers operate in cycles—feast and famine, windfall and drought. The illusion of freedom often obscures the underlying truth: volatility demands more discipline, not less. The Five-Bucket Budget, when adapted carefully, becomes not just a money management tool, but a stabilising philosophy for individuals who must make decisions under conditions of uncertainty.

Cash flow volatility is not merely inconvenient; it is psychologically destabilising. Research in behavioural economics has shown that irregular income increases financial anxiety, weakens self-control, and makes long-term planning more difficult—even when average income is higher than that of salaried peers. Entrepreneurs, consultants, creatives, and gig workers live with this tension constantly: how to spend today when tomorrow's income is a question mark. Traditional budgets, which assume a linear income stream, crumble under this pressure. The Five-Bucket model offers an alternative by reframing income not as a flow to be matched month by month, but as a resource to be buffered, paced, and intentionally distributed.

The key adaptation is to *de-link income from lifestyle*. In a salaried environment, people often budget reactively—spending or saving based on that month's pay. For the self-employed, this approach is dangerous. The first shift is psychological: income is not monthly; it is episodic. Thus, the budgeting system must run on *distributions*, not deposits. Think of it as running your personal finances like a well-managed company. Businesses with volatile revenues don't shut down in slow months—they maintain operating reserves and distribute profits on a set schedule. Your buckets function the same way.

To do this, one must first create a *Revenue Holding Tank*—a staging area, ideally a separate account, where all incoming funds are received but not yet allocated. From this tank, you transfer a fixed, sustainable amount—monthly or biweekly—into your Five-Bucket system. The goal is to create *income regularity artificially*. This is not a trick; it is a design decision. Even if you invoice £8,000 one month and £2,000 the next, your lifestyle draw might remain at £3,500 consistently, based on an average across the last six to twelve months. You pay yourself stability and let the volatility reside in the background.

Within this framework, the Five Buckets—Needs, Future, Safety, Joy, and Overflow—can now operate as intended. You are not forced to re-juggle proportions every time a payment arrives. Instead, you run your buckets on a dependable rhythm, adjusting only when long-term patterns shift. This predictability reduces stress, curbs reactive behaviour, and allows for true financial planning.

Let's turn to each bucket through the lens of entrepreneurial volatility. The *Needs* bucket—covering essentials like rent, utilities, and groceries—should be funded first and most conservatively. For freelancers, the margin for error is smaller, so this category may temporarily absorb a higher percentage of your staged draw. A 60% allocation in early phases is not excessive; it's protective. As your buffer grows, you can recalibrate.

The *Future* bucket—your investment in growth, retirement, or major goals—must reflect both vision and timing. For salaried workers, this bucket often functions as a quiet transfer into pensions or ISAs. For entrepreneurs, it may also include reinvestment into your business, skill development, or professional tools. But caution is key. Many freelancers fall into the trap of treating all spending as "investment," justifying laptops, courses, or branding as

Future-oriented when they're actually Joy disguised as productivity. Label honestly, and contribute strategically.

The *Safety* bucket is not optional—it is foundational. For irregular earners, this bucket is your stress buffer, your bridge across slow quarters, your insurance against sudden expenses. While the traditional advice is to hold 3–6 months of expenses in cash, self-employed individuals should aim for 6–12. This is not pessimism—it is *resilience engineering*. Each pound in Safety is a vote for your long-term survival. And its presence enables you to take calculated risks elsewhere.

The *Joy* bucket remains essential, though its role may need redefinition. Joy doesn't mean indulgence—it means intentional enjoyment. If your business has lean months, you may think the Joy bucket is expendable. But completely removing pleasure corrodes discipline. A better strategy is to *scale joy, don't erase it*. A dinner out becomes a home-cooked celebration. A getaway becomes a local day trip. Maintain the ritual of rewarding yourself within constraints. It reminds you that frugality is not deprivation—it is sovereignty.

Overflow, the final bucket, acts as both thermometer and opportunity scanner. When you have consistent surpluses in your holding tank, you have optionality: pay down debt, increase Safety, boost Joy, or invest in future projects. But use this signal wisely. Overflow doesn't mean your income is now stable—it means your system is working. Keep

Overflow flexible. Its job is to reveal patterns, not fund assumptions.

Tools can help implement this with less friction. Digital banking apps that allow multiple named sub-accounts—such as Monzo, Starling, or Revolut—let you visually emulate the buckets. But more important than the tool is the *cadence*. Choose a review frequency that matches your income rhythm. For some, weekly bucket check-ins provide the right sense of control. For others, a monthly reconciliation works better. The point is to replace chaos with structure, not to punish spontaneity. Your goal is to manage volatility with grace, not suppress it.

Tax obligations require special handling. Unlike salaried employees whose taxes are withheld automatically, self-employed individuals must proactively prepare for tax liabilities. The safest route is to treat taxes as a *sixth pseudo-bucket*—calculated as a percentage of gross income and held separately. This amount should never enter the spending equation. It is not yours. Automating this withholding to a dedicated tax account is the highest-yield behaviour for reducing future regret.

Mindset matters as much as mechanics. Irregular income doesn't mean you are financially unstable—it means your financial strategy must be *deliberately constructed*. Many freelancers oscillate between guilt in abundance and shame in scarcity. The Five-Bucket system removes the drama. It introduces rhythm. It gives your money structure, even when your calendar doesn't. And it lets you answer the question, “Can I afford this?” not based on today’s balance, but on your intentional design.

Too many self-employed people conflate freedom with chaos. The irony is that discipline expands freedom. By implementing a structured system like the Five Buckets, you reduce decision fatigue, improve clarity, and elevate your financial conversations—from internal panic to strategic insight. This is not just budgeting; it is executive function for your livelihood.

Finally, recognise that your buckets will evolve. A consultant in their first year may overallocate to Safety and underfund Joy. Five years later, they may tilt toward Future as their brand matures. Let the model breathe. But keep its spine intact: earning with unpredictability does not mean living reactively. The goal is not to escape volatility—it is to absorb it with intention, allocate it with clarity, and grow despite it. The Five Buckets don’t flatten your entrepreneurial journey—they furnish it with stability, so you can actually enjoy the ride.

For Caregivers and the Sandwich Generation: Budgeting Under the Weight of Shared Responsibility

The average adult in their 40s today is not merely planning for their future—they are managing the financial present of at least two other generations. Caught between ageing parents and dependent children, many find themselves navigating a tri-directional pull on their time, income, and emotional bandwidth. This demographic, often referred to as the "sandwich generation," is growing fast—and its members are under-supported by traditional budgeting advice that assumes autonomy and singular financial purpose. In reality, these individuals are managing multiple lives through a single paycheque, and their success hinges not on earnings alone, but on precision, resilience, and systems-level thinking.

The Five-Bucket Budget is uniquely suited to this complexity because it resists the false promise of "balance" and instead offers a model for *prioritised clarity*. In situations where income is fixed and demands are elastic, what matters most is not perfect distribution, but conscious trade-offs. The truth is stark: when you are financially responsible for others, budgeting is no longer about optimisation—it becomes a form of triage. But triage does not mean chaos. It means structured, values-aligned decision-making under pressure. The five-bucket approach provides that scaffolding.

The challenge begins with the Needs bucket, which in most households under strain begins to balloon disproportionately. Needs expand when you're paying for school uniforms and subsidising your father's medications. What once fit into 50% of income might now demand 70%, leaving little room for Joy or Future planning. The reflex is to feel failure. But the more constructive path is to *redraw the boundary of what counts as a 'need'*. This requires ruthless honesty. A third streaming subscription may be emotionally comforting, but it is not non-negotiable. By formally categorising expenses—both your own and those of dependents—you begin to detect discretionary choices hiding under the cloak of obligation.

This is especially true in multigenerational households, where interdependence blurs the lines between generosity and necessity. Are you paying your mother's utility bill out of duty or because she genuinely cannot afford it? Is the family takeaway every weekend a joyful ritual or an avoidance of deeper budget conversations? These aren't just financial questions—they are emotional diagnostics. The Five-Bucket system forces visibility. It externalises assumptions. And in doing so, it becomes not just a budgeting tool but a family communication protocol.

To use it effectively, caregivers must start with a *shared reality map*. This means itemising every source of income and every category of responsibility—children's costs, parental medical bills, household operations—without judgement. The goal is not to eliminate emotions but to *contain them inside structure*. You cannot budget effectively for others until you know what you're actually subsidising. And often, families are shocked by the mismatch between perceived burdens and actual expenditures. One adult child may think they're carrying the lion's share of parental support, only to find their sibling's contributions are simply less visible. Structure fosters transparency. And transparency reduces resentment.

The Safety bucket becomes existential in this context. A caregiver with no emergency fund is not just financially vulnerable—they are perpetually one crisis away from collapse. Ironically, this is the bucket most often sacrificed under strain. The logic is understandable: why save £200 when your child's dentist bill is £180? But the result is long-term instability. A functioning Safety bucket, even if it grows slowly, creates the psychological breathing room to make non-reactive choices. For many sandwich generation earners, *automating even a small, fixed monthly transfer to Safety is a non-negotiable act of self-protection*. It signals that your future matters too.

The Joy bucket presents a paradox. It is often viewed as indulgent when caring for others. Parents forgo hobbies, date nights, even haircuts to funnel resources to dependents. But erasing Joy leads to burnout—and burnout degrades decision-making. A sustainable caregiving system must include pleasure. Not extravagance—pleasure. Something weekly. Predictable. Affordable. Joy becomes functional when it is deliberately chosen, rather than guiltily stolen. It also sets a model: children raised in environments where adults prioritise modest self-care grow into adults who understand boundaries. So too with ageing parents. Many resist "being a burden" but feel confused when their children are perpetually harried and joyless. A consistent Joy bucket, however small, becomes an anchor for psychological durability.

Overflow is unlikely to appear frequently for caregivers—but when it does, it should be treated with reverence. A tax refund, small bonus, or gift should not be absorbed into the vortex of everyday need without pause. Instead, it becomes a diagnostic moment: *Where is the system most strained?* Is it Safety that needs reinforcement? Has Joy been running on empty? Should a Future goal—retirement, upskilling, relocation—be accelerated? Overflow becomes not just a reward but an X-ray. It tells you where the pressure has built up quietly, waiting for a release valve.

The most challenging bucket for caregivers, however, is Future. It is the easiest to defer. After all, retirement is 20 years away—your son's tuition is 20 days away. But this deferral, repeated for a decade, becomes structural sacrifice. A sustainable budget must carry your future within its present. This is not just about pensions or savings; it is about dignity. Every pound you invest in your own future reduces the likelihood of becoming a burden to the very people you're now supporting. This is the long arc of intergenerational responsibility. *Caring for others now should not require the forfeiture of your eventual autonomy.*

One of the most overlooked techniques for those supporting others financially is *percentage-based partitioning*. Instead of trying to meet every demand fully or arbitrarily, allocate fixed percentages of your total income to each of the five buckets and then *negotiate needs to fit those ratios*. This shifts the locus of decision-making from "What can we afford?" to "What are we prioritising inside our constraints?" This approach is more psychologically protective. It limits decision fatigue and preserves a sense of agency, even when resources are constrained.

Technology can also assist. Use of banking features such as auto-splitting deposits into multiple named accounts or "pots" can reduce the friction of bucket management. So too can shared digital spreadsheets or apps that allow multiple contributors—particularly helpful for siblings jointly caring for parents. Transparency across a shared framework prevents duplication, diffuses resentment, and makes invisible labour visible.

Perhaps the most difficult skill caregivers must master is *graceful boundary-setting*. The Five-Bucket model provides not only a financial map, but a script for saying no with clarity. If your Joy bucket is empty this month, you can tell your teenager that the trip to the cinema must wait—not because you're stingy or tired, but because your budget is built to protect everyone. If your Safety bucket needs a top-up, you can decline a family loan request without shame, pointing to the structure, not the sentiment. This is not a model of scarcity—it is a model of principled stewardship.

Caregiving, at its core, is the act of investing in others without draining oneself entirely. Budgeting, in this context, is not just arithmetic—it is philosophy. It is the disciplined assertion that responsibility should be shared, that dignity matters on all sides, and that your well-being is not a luxury, but a prerequisite for sustainable care. The Five-Bucket model gives caregivers something rare: a language for complexity, a framework for fairness, and a method for enduring what others may never fully understand.

There is no perfect ratio for budgeting across three generations. There is only intentionality, iteration, and honesty. The Five-Bucket system cannot erase the burdens of the sandwich generation, but it can redistribute them across time, categories, and meaning. It lets you see your life as a system—not a scramble. And in a world that rarely makes space for those carrying more than their share, that clarity is not just helpful. It is radical.

Chapter 10
When Things Break—And How to Rebuild

Financial collapse is rarely about money alone. It touches identity, safety, trust, control—and, most sharply, shame. A lost job, an overdrawn card, an emergency that overwhelms your reserves: these are not mere line items on a spreadsheet; they are seismic jolts to one's sense of self. They shake not only bank balances but narratives—who we think we are, how we arrived here, whether we are still capable of moving forward. Conventional personal finance texts tend to dwell on strategy, but the deeper truth is this: a system cannot be rebuilt if you cannot face it without shame. That is the hidden weight of financial collapse—not the numbers themselves, but the silence and avoidance they inspire.

Society scripts our responses to mistakes in familiar ways: denial, deflection, delay. Confession, when it comes, often carries self-punishment, a belief that public humiliation somehow restores credibility. None of it aids recovery. Every system fails at some point; even the most financially literate can be undone by illness, poor timing, relational upheaval, or misjudged risk. The skill worth cultivating is not infallibility, but the art of failing well. That is the premise of this chapter.

We start by unpacking the emotional architecture of financial failure. Why do thoughtful, capable individuals freeze at the sight of an overdraft notice? Why do couples quarrel more fiercely over a missed bill than over chronic illness or grief? Why does a single misstep feel like a moral failing rather than a logistical hiccup? These are not trivial questions. Financial decisions are laden with symbolism and emotion; recognising that weight is the first step toward liberation.

Once that recognition occurs, tools can follow. The Five-Bucket Budget is not merely a growth framework; it becomes a scaffold for regaining control. In moments of collapse, the buckets shift in significance. Needs must be defined with ruthless clarity. Joy may be reduced, but it cannot vanish—dignity and mental resilience matter even in crisis. Safety ascends to the highest priority, even if rebuilding takes months. Overflow, if it appears, becomes triage fuel rather than indulgence. The Future bucket, once aspirational, transforms into a testament to stubborn hope—proof that planning continues despite adversity.

This chapter includes an unusual element in financial literature: a case study of recovery rather than triumph. We trace the real-world experience of an individual who filed for bankruptcy and rebuilt their financial life using the five-bucket method—not through windfalls or miraculous reversals, but through steady adaptation, consistency, and recalibrated measures of success. This story is not a tale of luck; it is evidence that repair is possible, and that structure can coexist with despair without waiting for optimism to arrive first.

Perhaps the most counterintuitive lesson is this: repair is not weakness—it is competence. In engineering, medicine, or relationships, we accept system failure and design for repair. In personal finance, we expect infallibility, a framing that is both unrealistic and cruel. What if financial health were measured not by uninterrupted success but by the robustness of a protocol for returning to baseline? This chapter invites you to adopt that perspective. Relapse is not a character judgment; it is a natural aspect of a flexible, functional system.

Breakdowns will occur. This is not a hypothetical to fear, but a reality to prepare for. A budget's value is tested not in smooth times, but in its ability to be reconstructed under strain. The Five-Bucket framework is designed with that resilience at its core. By the chapter's end, the aim is clear: not only to navigate financial setbacks, but to emerge from them calmer, wiser, and equipped with a system capable of bending without breaking. When things fail, the true question is no longer, "Why did this happen?" but rather, "What will I do next, and how will I reclaim it?"

The Psychology of Financial Setbacks

Few things in adult life feel as deeply personal—and publicly humiliating—as a financial mistake. Whether it's missing a mortgage payment, maxing out a credit card, or watching a business venture collapse, the blow is rarely contained to numbers on a screen. It strikes our sense of identity. Of competence. Of safety. The emotional aftershocks can be more destabilising than the monetary loss itself, particularly in a culture where financial status doubles as moral standing. This is not merely unfortunate. It is dangerous—because when people internalise their financial missteps as personal failings, they become less likely to recover. *Shame does not fuel correction; it fuels paralysis.*

To understand why so many smart, capable individuals freeze in the face of financial setbacks, we must first unpick the wiring of the human response to failure. Psychologists describe three primary modes of response under acute psychological distress: fight, flight, and freeze. While "fight" and "flight" still imply movement—however misdirected—*freeze* renders the individual inert. In financial terms, this can mean unopened bills, avoided phone calls, neglected bank apps. Rationally, we know that avoidance exacerbates the damage. Yet rationality is rarely the operative system in such moments. What takes over is *affect*: the raw, unfiltered weight of emotion, fear, and identity threat.

This is compounded by the illusion of control we are sold through mainstream personal finance advice. Much of the dominant literature implies that wealth is simply a function of willpower and knowledge. Save more, spend less, invest wisely. If you're in trouble, it's because you weren't disciplined enough. But this framing is not only inaccurate—it is cruel. It ignores structural realities like income volatility, medical emergencies, wage stagnation, and caregiving burdens. More insidiously, it burdens the individual with full accountability for an outcome over which they may have had only partial control. *The result is internalised blame that masquerades as moral truth.*

Shame, unlike guilt, is not about what you did—it's about who you are. And when people believe their financial missteps are reflective of inherent incompetence, they do not seek tools; they seek cover. They shrink from conversations, ignore resources, and isolate themselves. This is not a personality defect—it is a coping mechanism. But it is one that must be interrupted, and that interruption begins with *normalisation*. Every single person who manages money over time will get something wrong. Most will get many things wrong. This is not proof of inadequacy; it is proof of participation. The only people who never make money mistakes are the ones who aren't engaged with the system at all—or who are insulated from its consequences by unearned privilege.

Reframing financial setbacks requires more than empathy—it requires architecture. People need models, scripts, and systems that do not rely on uninterrupted success. The Five-Bucket Budget system is particularly suited to this challenge because it is inherently dynamic. It does not expect perfection; it expects fluctuation. When someone experiences a setback, they do not need to abandon the structure—they can reconfigure within it. For instance, if income drops, the *Future* bucket may be temporarily paused, while *Needs* and *Safety* receive priority. The *Joy* bucket can be preserved at a minimal level to maintain psychological continuity, and *Overflow* is redefined as emotional rather than financial surplus—any act of re-engagement, however small, counts.

This ability to *stay within the system even when the numbers fall short* is profoundly therapeutic. It reinforces agency without demanding immediate results. It tells the individual: "You are still participating. You have not failed. You are adjusting." That shift—*from failure to adjustment*—is the psychological linchpin of recovery. Behavioural science supports this approach. Research in habit formation, particularly the work of B.J. Fogg and James Clear, has shown that identity-aligned micro-actions are more sustainable than drastic interventions. In plain terms, small steps taken consistently beat radical plans abandoned quickly. Especially in the aftermath of a setback, individuals need friction-reducing cues to take action, not aspirational mantras that require perfect conditions.

Case studies confirm this. Consider a single mother who, after a divorce, found herself with £1,200 in overdraft and no financial plan. Traditional advice would have pushed her to cancel subscriptions, hustle for side gigs, and restrict discretionary spending to zero. Instead, she implemented a simplified version of the Five-Bucket system. She automated a modest weekly transfer into a *Safety* reserve, set a calendar reminder to review her balances on Sundays, and allocated £5 per week to a *Joy* bucket for coffee and books—rituals that helped her feel intact. Within three months, she was out of overdraft. Within six months, she was saving. But the real win was psychological: she no longer described herself as "bad with money." She described herself as "in motion."

Another crucial psychological shift comes from the reframing of time. Financial trauma distorts our sense of temporality. A single bad month can feel like a permanent state. A mistake feels defining. To counter this, people need future-looking practices that do not feel performative. One effective method is to reintroduce *checkpoints* rather than goals. Instead of aiming to "be financially stable by next year," individuals can adopt checkpoints like "review my Needs and Safety allocations on the 15th of each month" or "resume Joy spending at 1% of income once overdraft is cleared." These are not about performance; they are about presence. *They reinforce that the individual is still a participant in their financial life, even when progress is invisible.*

There is also a relational dimension to financial shame. It often breeds secrecy in partnerships, distance in friendships, and avoidance in professional contexts. Here, normalisation must be social, not just internal. Thoughtful communication scripts can help. Rather than saying, "I messed up and I don't want to talk about it," a person might say, "I'm in the middle of a financial reset and still figuring things out—thanks for giving me space while I sort it." This isn't just semantics; it's sovereignty. It maintains dignity while acknowledging flux. Over time, this kind of communication models resilience for others and reduces the stigma around cyclical financial recovery.

Of course, not every setback is psychological in nature—some are structural. When the income stream dries up, or medical debt escalates, or a dependent family member's care costs spike, emotional insight alone is insufficient. But it is still necessary. Because the difference between someone who takes constructive action and someone who collapses further is not just about access—it is about *activation*. People must believe they are worth the effort of recovery. They must believe their situation is redeemable. No budget—however brilliant—can override the deadweight of hopelessness. Which is why every financial system must come embedded with its own repair logic.

This is where the Five-Bucket method quietly excels. Unlike conventional zero-based budgets or restrictive envelopes, it contains room for adaptation, fluidity, and personal pacing. The buckets do not demand equal attention at all times. They respond to circumstances. They can shrink, pause, prioritise, and restart—without judgment. That flexibility is not just practical; it is *psychologically humane*. It offers people the space to be human—to break, regroup, and begin again.

Ultimately, the true measure of financial maturity is not how well one avoids mistakes—it is how one *responds* to them. That response must begin with language: the internal monologue that either condemns or supports. By naming financial setbacks not as shameful aberrations but as inevitable variables in a complex system, we reclaim the narrative. And in doing so, we enable people not just to bounce back, but to build forward—anchored not in guilt, but in clarity, structure, and self-respect.

Using the Buckets to Regain Control

Financial disruption rarely arrives politely. It doesn't ask for your permission or check your calendar. It tears through with the force of sudden job loss, medical emergency, or a bout of overspending that was meant to be a "one-time thing." In these moments, conventional budgeting advice quickly collapses under the weight of real life. There is little comfort in being told to "cut expenses" when the fridge is already empty, or to "tap your emergency fund" when the emergency has already bled it dry. And yet, amid the fog of financial chaos, there remains one critical truth: *the fastest way to regain agency is not through willpower, but through structure*. Not rigid spreadsheets or punitive tracking—but a responsive, psychologically attuned system. This is where the Five-Bucket Budget proves itself not as a peacetime luxury, but as a wartime strategy.

The essential value of the bucket framework in moments of breakdown is that it provides clarity without requiring perfection. It doesn't assume a fixed income or predictable rhythm. It accommodates volatility, reprioritisation, and pauses. And perhaps most importantly, it offers a way to *reset without starting over*. When your finances are in disarray, the goal is not to reconstruct the ideal plan you once had. The goal is to stabilise the now—to make your next financial decision not out of panic, but from a place of anchored logic.

The first task is diagnostic. Not all financial setbacks are the same, and therefore not all responses should be. A job loss is different from a reckless overspend. A caregiving emergency differs from a failed investment. *The cause matters, because it determines which lever to pull first.* Begin by answering one question: Is this a *temporary shock* or an *ongoing condition*? If temporary—such as a missed freelance payment or one-off car repair—the objective is containment and triage. If ongoing—such as chronic underemployment or rising long-term costs—the objective is structural adjustment. Both paths require a system, but they differ in rhythm and focus.

Let's take the acute scenario first: a one-time setback that throws your budget into crisis mode. The instinctive response is to halt all spending, freeze every account, and live in austerity. But that rarely sustains. Instead, shift to what we might call a *stabilisation mode* using the buckets. The *Needs* bucket becomes your immediate command centre. Inventory what must be paid this week and next—housing, food, transport—and redirect all available funds here. This is not about budgeting—it's about operational survival. Simultaneously, pause discretionary allocations to *Future* (long-term goals) and *Overflow* (surplus investments). These are not abandoned—only suspended.

But here is the psychological counterintuitive twist: *do not eliminate your Joy bucket completely*. Even in financial triage, preserving a modest allowance—say £5 a week—for a small ritual (a coffee, a book, a creative tool) keeps you psychologically engaged with your own wellbeing. This is not indulgence. It is strategic morale maintenance. Behavioural research consistently shows that systems which preserve even tiny moments of autonomy are more durable under stress.

If the crisis is more chronic—such as six months of inconsistent income or supporting an ailing parent—the buckets must be rebalanced. Here, you need to formalise the fluidity. Convert irregular income into a rolling average—take the last three months, identify the lowest earning month, and treat that as your baseline. You are not budgeting for best-case scenarios. You are budgeting for resilience. From this base, build a provisional allocation: *Needs* get funded first, followed by *Safety*—the reserve that protects against further dips. *Future* goals may need to be delayed, but should not be deleted. Even a £10 contribution per month toward a long-term aim sustains a sense of forward motion.

There is also a case to be made for reverse budgeting during crisis: instead of allocating based on income, you allocate based on minimum viable costs. What's the bare minimum required to maintain housing, nutrition, and health? Once this is calculated, it becomes your *Survival Operating Budget*. Any income above this threshold can then be assigned using traditional bucket logic. This creates a powerful psychological shift: *you move from guessing and hoping to knowing and deciding*. That agency is what most people lack in the wake of financial shock—not just money, but a method to make sense of the remaining money.

Let us consider a real-world case: a mid-career professional who loses their job unexpectedly, with only two months' severance and a mortgage to pay. Panic sets in. The savings account, once vaguely intended for retirement, is now their only buffer. Without a system, they might drain it emotionally—using large unplanned withdrawals driven by fear or guilt. With the bucket method, however, they divide the lump sum into proportional buckets—£5,000 total becomes £2,500 in *Needs*, £1,000 in *Safety*, £500 in *Joy*, and £1,000 in *Future* (paused). Each category is treated with precision. Weekly spending is drawn from Needs, and all other buckets are temporarily frozen with scheduled reviews. The Joy allocation, while small, is crucial: it allows for a Friday night takeaway or a birthday gift—humanising the experience of unemployment. The result? Panic is replaced by pacing.

Beyond the mechanics, there is a deeper lesson: *a good system does not prevent breakdowns—it gives you the ability to rebuild without losing yourself.* One of the most overlooked effects of financial hardship is identity erosion. People go from "provider" to "burden," from "planner" to "problem." The bucket system subtly protects against this by maintaining roles, structure, and a sense of authorship. Even when income drops to near zero, the act of making conscious, compartmentalised choices—this £20 for medicine, this £10 for a child's toy, this £5 for coffee—reminds the individual that they are still making decisions, not simply enduring consequences.

This also holds true after an overspending episode. Unlike an external crisis, overspending triggers guilt and self-recrimination. The instinct is to "punish" oneself by cutting everything. This is both ineffective and unnecessary.

Instead, use the buckets to *audit the pattern* that led to the breach. Was the overspend in Needs (misjudged essential expenses), Joy (emotional spending), or Future (overcommitted giving or investing)? Once the root is identified, recalibrate. If Joy spending was the culprit, do not eliminate it—reduce and reassign. If Needs were underestimated, revise your assumptions. A 5–10% rebalance across categories can restore order within a week. This isn't discipline—it's design.

One of the quiet powers of the bucket framework is its built-in review mechanism. After any disruption—whether large or small—schedule a reset review. A 30-minute session where you:

Review your current bucket balances

Assess current vs. desired allocations based on new income data

Reactivate or adjust suspended buckets

This becomes a ritual of re-entry—a practical, dignified way of returning to order. And once repeated, it forms a psychological anchor: "This is how I recover. This is what I do when things go wrong."

Financial systems are often judged by how well they work under ideal conditions. But the true test is how they function under strain. A good system doesn't require you to be your best self to be useful. It meets you where you are and helps you move, gradually, to a place of better stability.

The Five-Bucket model, when used not just to manage wealth but to weather instability, becomes more than a budgeting tool—it becomes a *resilience framework*. It helps translate chaos into categories, emotion into action, and fear into a strategy.

Ultimately, the goal is not just to regain control of your money. It is to regain control of your narrative. And that begins—not with sweeping resolutions—but with one decisive, categorised choice. Then another. And another. *Control returns in increments, not declarations.* And with each step, you remind yourself: this system works not because I never falter—but because it knows exactly how to carry me when I do.

Case Study: From Bankruptcy to Balance

The numbers were no longer abstract. They arrived in brown envelopes, stamped urgent, demanding responses not in theory but in cash. When Lydia filed for bankruptcy at age 43, it wasn't because she had misread a spreadsheet or failed to understand interest rates. It was because life had compounded: a divorce, a redundancy, a few years of self-employment that never quite covered the bills, and a terminally ill parent whose care costs fell silently but steadily on her shoulders. Her story is not unique, which is precisely why it matters. *What distinguishes Lydia's journey is not the collapse, but the method by which she rebuilt.* That method was the Five-Bucket Budget.

Bankruptcy is not just a legal event—it's a cognitive rupture. It severs one's perceived connection to financial competence and replaces it with a narrative of failure. Lydia described it as "a sort of quiet erasure"—she went from being someone who made choices about money to someone who avoided the topic entirely. When she first encountered the Five-Bucket framework, she was sceptical. "I didn't want a system. I wanted absolution." But what she found was more useful than comfort: *a means of re-entry.*

Her income post-bankruptcy was modest and erratic. A part-time admin role brought in £1,200 per month, supplemented by sporadic weekend childcare jobs. Her fixed expenses—rent, transport, utilities—consumed over 70% of that. Traditional budgeting models encouraged her to "cut discretionary spending," but that wasn't a solution—it was a punishment. The bucket model presented an alternative: *allocate by purpose, not pressure.*

The initial step was not technical but emotional. She needed to *re-establish agency,* and that meant deciding where her money would go before it disappeared. Using a simple notebook, she created her own version of the buckets:

Needs: rent, groceries, utilities, phone

Safety: a slowly growing buffer—£10 per week at first

Joy: capped at £5, often used for a café breakfast on Sundays

Future: debt repayment and a long-view savings goal

Overflow: temporarily suspended, but marked for future use

What struck Lydia was not the brilliance of the model, but its *permission to be human*. Her Joy bucket, though small, gave her psychological buoyancy. The Future bucket—used not for retirement but for small debt repayments—transformed a shameful obligation into a measurable commitment. Her Safety bucket became a game: could she add just a little more this week than last? Within six months, her mindset had shifted from scarcity to strategy. Within twelve, she had three months' worth of rent saved. *Structure gave her traction. Traction restored her confidence.*

One of the most pivotal moments came when she received a tax refund of £850. Pre-bucket Lydia would have used it to extinguish panic. Bucket Lydia treated it as a *rebalancing opportunity*. She split it as follows:

£400 to Safety (building her buffer)

£200 to Future (paying off a high-interest credit card)

£100 to Joy (a short train trip to visit her sister)

£100 to Needs (forward-paying her electricity bill)

£50 to Overflow (now slowly reactivated)

The process was not just about amounts. It was about *affirming priorities under pressure*. Each allocation became a statement: "I may have filed for bankruptcy, but I am not broken. I am still designing my life." That insight is not unique to Lydia—it is inherent in the bucket structure itself. By requiring conscious separation of financial purposes, the model trains the mind to think in terms of agency rather than aftermath.

Lydia's journey was not linear. There were setbacks: a winter boiler repair that drained her Safety bucket, an impulse purchase that sent Joy into overdraft. But because each bucket was contained, the fallout was localised. There was no catastrophic chain reaction. *This compartmentalisation is one of the quiet superpowers of the framework*—it transforms what might be existential into what is simply logistical.

Over time, Lydia noticed a deeper transformation. She began talking about money—not as an apology, but as a subject. She taught her teenage daughter the bucket method using coloured jars on a windowsill. She joined a local mutual aid group, not for help but to offer budgeting workshops to others in transition. *Recovery became not just personal but participatory.*

It would be facile to reduce Lydia's recovery to a budgeting tool. What mattered more was that the tool respected her complexity. It didn't demand perfection. It didn't punish missteps. It simply provided a container—a set of vessels into which she could pour small, repeated efforts. That accumulation of micro-decisions became, over time, *a scaffold for stability*.

There is a tendency in financial literature to glorify success stories that end in wealth. But the more instructive stories are those that result in balance, dignity, and *sustained authorship over one's economic life*. Lydia never became rich. But she became *anchored*. Her finances are now boring, in the best possible sense. The phone no longer rings with creditors. The envelopes are now newsletters, not warnings. She no longer avoids her bank app; she checks it every Saturday morning, coffee in hand, buckets in mind.

Her case reminds us that recovery is not about making one heroic choice—it's about designing an environment in which even vulnerable people can make strong decisions consistently. The Five-Bucket Budget was not a lifeboat for Lydia. It was the shoreline—clearly marked, patiently waiting, structured so she could land safely, stand up again, and begin to move forward.

To rebuild after collapse requires more than discipline. It requires design. And in that design, every bucket becomes not just a container of cash, but a symbol of care, clarity, and conscious living.

Why Repair Is a Superpower

Financial culture often lionises the unbroken—the debt-free graduate, the first-time homeowner at twenty-eight, the startup founder who never misstepped. But the more instructive stories, and the more common human experience, are those that involve deviation and return. Everyone miscalculates, overspends, under-earns, or gets blindsided. What separates sustainable financial wellbeing from chronic struggle isn't a flawless record—it's *the capacity to repair*. That ability is neither trivial nor secondary. *It is the defining skill of financial maturity.*

At the heart of this redefinition lies a philosophical tension: the popular narrative of fiscal success is built on continuity, but real life is built on interruption. We lose jobs. We support ill relatives. We make decisions under stress. These aren't anomalies; they are recurring features of adult life. Yet our financial systems—both formal and social—rarely honour recovery. Credit scores penalise lapses without recognising course corrections. Workplace culture rewards unbroken progress but seldom celebrates resilience. The result is a silent epidemic: people who believe they've failed not because they overspent, but because they think they're *the kind of person who overspends*.

This is where the Five-Bucket model becomes more than a budgeting method. It becomes *a repair manual*. Not because it reverses mistakes instantly, but because it offers a pathway forward without shame. When your buckets fall out of alignment—perhaps your Safety bucket is drained or your Joy bucket has overflowed into credit—you aren't stuck in purgatory. You have structure. You know what's next. *The process of rebuilding becomes intelligible and finite.*

Consider someone who's just experienced a financial shock: a car accident, a medical bill, or a dry quarter in freelance income. The typical emotional response isn't just concern—it's collapse. We freeze. We tell ourselves stories: "I've ruined everything," "I'm back to square one," "I'm just bad with money." These narratives are not facts; they are responses to disorientation. Repair begins with replacing narrative distortion with clarity of process. The buckets do this by reframing money as a set of functions—not moral verdicts.

One of the most powerful features of the system is that it's inherently self-correcting. If your Overflow bucket is empty, that doesn't mean you're indulgent. It means your inputs have changed. If your Needs bucket is consuming 90% of your income, that doesn't make you irresponsible. It makes visible a constraint you must now problem-solve. *Every imbalance is data. Repair begins with observation, not judgement.*

In practice, repair often starts small. A single week of returning to your default allocations, even in partial amounts, restores a sense of authorship. Perhaps you can't fund all five buckets, but you can fund three. Perhaps your Safety bucket is paused, but your Joy bucket gets a modest infusion—enough to remind you that life continues. *These are not trivial acts; they are declarations of capability.* You are saying, "I am still in charge of where this goes."

Psychologically, this is profound. Research in behavioural science confirms that people are more likely to make future-oriented decisions when they feel effective in the present. The buckets reinforce this by enabling micro-repairs. You don't have to "get your finances back on track" in one heroic move. You simply move £20 into Future, or ring-fence a small portion of income for Joy. *Momentum replaces perfection as the currency of progress.*

This reframing has implications beyond personal finance. Culturally, we are hungry for models that allow failure without catastrophe. We want systems that absorb human error. The Five-Bucket method does not offer immunity from disruption, but it *normalises recovery as a regular function*. It bakes grace into its structure. There is no special procedure for a reset; the framework is built to be resumed.

In a society obsessed with scale—bigger incomes, bigger investments, bigger payoffs—repair reminds us that *continuity is not the same as health*. A flawless-looking financial life may be fragile, propped up by denial or debt. A life that stumbles but recovers is *anti-fragile*—stronger for its stress tests. The skill of repair allows people to engage risk, take initiative, and make generous decisions without the existential fear of one wrong move ruining everything.

This is not a call for recklessness. It is a call for *compassionate accountability*. A system that expects people to behave perfectly is not humane—it's naïve. Adults, especially those supporting families or facing systemic constraints, will deviate from plan. The point is not to prevent deviation at all costs, but to *build environments where returning is easier than disappearing*. The buckets, with their specificity and modularity, make return frictionless.

The final—and perhaps most overlooked—benefit of repair is that it builds trust. Not in abstract systems, but in the self. Each time someone notices a bucket off-balance and takes action, they send themselves a message: "I can course-correct." Over time, this becomes an internalised belief. And with that belief, behaviour changes. Budgets get reviewed, even when they're imperfect. Conversations about money get initiated, even when they're uncomfortable. Opportunities get pursued, even when success is not guaranteed. *Repair generates initiative.*

This capacity is invaluable in households. Partners who trust in their own and each other's ability to recover are less reactive and more constructive during financial stress. Parents who model repair teach children that responsibility includes recovery, not just restraint. Communities that embrace economic repair over economic punishment foster inclusion, not exclusion. In short, *repair is relational as much as it is fiscal.*

The prevailing myth of financial success is that it is a line trending ever upward. But real financial lives are full of U-turns, pauses, plateaus, and pivots. By defining success as the *ability to return*—to re-engage with intention after disruption—we shift the frame from purity to practice. That shift is not just intellectually honest; it is practically liberating.

What the Five-Bucket model ultimately offers is not merely order, but *a method for re-ordering*. The buckets hold more than money; they hold memory. When we return to them after a setback, we are not starting from zero. We are returning to a known landscape, one that carries the imprint of our prior care. And that return—that quiet, self-directed, resolute return—is the very definition of power.

To be able to repair is not to admit failure. It is to declare that nothing—not loss, not shame, not fear—gets the final word on what your financial life can become.

Chapter 11
The Map Is the Method

Most people do not stumble because they lack ambition. They falter because their systems cannot withstand the messiness of real life. Ask someone about their financial aspirations and they can usually articulate them: independence, security, a home, peace of mind, perhaps a comfortable retirement. Ask how they are operationalising that vision, though, and clarity often vanishes. The intention is there, but the scaffolding is absent. They navigate without a map and wonder why they keep circling the same terrain. The five-bucket model offers no miracles, but it does offer orientation. It cannot eliminate uncertainty or replace discipline. What it does is allow you, when life inevitably shifts, to reroute without losing your sense of direction.

The most pernicious myth in personal finance is that success hinges solely on willpower. Yet behavioural economics, with contributions from luminaries like Daniel Kahneman and Richard Thaler, repeatedly shows the limits of intention alone in complex systems. Financial missteps rarely stem from character flaws; they arise because goals are not embedded in structures that align daily behaviour with long-term aspiration. This is where the bucket framework excels: it turns vision into navigation. You need not reinvent yourself each time life throws a curveball—you merely recalculate within a familiar system.

This chapter challenges conventional definitions of progress. Many measure it in accumulation: more savings, fewer debts, rising net worth. Useful, yes, but they are lagging indicators—they report what has already occurred.

Alignment offers a richer metric: the consistency between daily behaviour and declared values. Someone who claims that family stability is paramount, yet devotes every spare hour to side projects at the expense of rest or presence, is misaligned. Another who prizes generosity but has not budgeted a penny for giving in twelve months is similarly off course. These are not moral failings; they are process misfires. Buckets illuminate such misalignments and invite recalibration.

Recalibration is not reactive; it is ritual. Resilient individuals do not wait for crises to course-correct. They schedule structured pauses—quiet moments to scan for drift. This is not obsession but maintenance. The distinction between a budget that collapses and one that endures is rarely intelligence or income; it is the presence of touchpoints. The five-bucket model provides them: a monthly glance at each category, a quarterly reflection, an annual review. Not bureaucratic box-ticking, but living, adaptive conversation. These rhythms transform budgeting from burden to compass.

This practice allows for a subtle yet profound capability: forgiveness without forgetfulness. A poor month does not erase a strong year. A failed quarter does not negate a decade of care. When each bucket is tracked over time, trends emerge without panic. Future may have been underfunded in February but overfunded in June; such variation is not failure, but adaptation. The five-bucket system builds memory into your finances. Like a seasoned hiker reading contours on a map, you learn where you have been and which adjustments matter most for the path ahead.

The chapter also reframes what counts as financial knowledge. Too often, people rely solely on external metrics: account balances, credit scores, spreadsheets. Important, yes—but incomplete. How you feel about your money matters too. Not in vague affirmations, but as a diagnostic. Tightness, anxiety, disorganisation—all are data points. Calm, clarity, and a sense of control are equally informative. Emotional cues often signal friction long before numbers do. When buckets are well-calibrated, the nervous system responds: you sleep better, replaying purchases less, confident that even a lean month is embedded in a plan. This is wealth you can feel.

Such psychological gains are far from soft metrics—they shape real outcomes. A clear, calm mind negotiates better, risks wisely, and rebounds swiftly from setbacks. Financial freedom, after all, is rarely about numbers alone; it is the absence of chronic, disorganising fear. The five-bucket framework provides this: clear containers for what is available, untouchable, delayed, or reserved for joy. It directs your money while liberating your mind.

The method also inoculates against the fragility of goal-based thinking. Goals are brittle: aim to save £5,000, and a boiler breaking can make that target feel absurd, prompting abandonment. With a map-like structure, you do not abandon; you reroute. That £5,000 may take longer, but you know which bucket the emergency drew from, and which must be refilled. You lose time, not strategy—a distinction that matters immensely.

Durability is crucial in complex lives: irregular income, caregiving roles, medical uncertainty, intergenerational support. Such circumstances demand systems that are simultaneously fixed and flexible. The buckets offer this. Categories remain stable; allocations adjust. Like a GPS, the system does not chastise a wrong turn—it reroutes.

Most importantly, this chapter reinterprets wealth itself. If wealth is defined solely by accumulation, few feel secure. If defined as clarity, adaptability, and psychological stability, it becomes accessible. Wealth is alignment between values and money. It is knowing that each pound has purpose, even when resources are lean. It is meeting life's surprises with process rather than panic.

The five-bucket method promises not perfection, but navigation. A map cannot guarantee calm seas or straight roads, but it ensures you do not wander aimlessly. With this system, progress is not chasing distant targets or shaming yourself for detours. It is orienting daily action toward a coherent, flexible vision—and staying in motion, even as the landscape shifts. With the method as your map, you do not start over: you check your bearings and continue.

From Goals to Navigation

Most people are not short on goals—they're overwhelmed by them. The challenge is rarely ambition; it is architecture. A person may say they want to "save more," "buy a house," "get out of debt," or "travel more freely," but strip those phrases of context and they reveal themselves for what they are: vague desires unmoored from structure. Goals that lack operational definition cannot be executed. They drift, wobble, and eventually dissolve in the daily noise of life. They are castles drawn in fog.

What undermines these intentions is not a lack of intelligence or discipline, but a flawed interface between human cognition and time. Behavioural science has long established that we tend to discount future outcomes—what psychologists call "hyperbolic discounting." The further away a reward appears, the less effort we're willing to apply today. Even deeply meaningful goals lose salience when competing with an overdue bill or an emotionally charged purchase. Traditional budgets often fail because they attempt to impose rigid control on a system that is fundamentally fluid. They assume linearity in a world that resists it. When the plan breaks—as it inevitably does—it invites shame, not iteration. This is the psychological pitfall of financial fragility: *if the plan must be perfect to be valid, then any deviation invalidates the plan*.

The five-bucket framework sidesteps this fragility by rejecting the fantasy of fixed paths. Instead of pinning all hope on brittle projections, it builds a durable navigational structure—closer to a GPS than a set of static directions. Your income flows into five distinct containers: Essentials, Future, Safety, Joy, and Freedom. Each bucket serves a specific purpose, and each receives a percentage-based allocation. You are no longer budgeting line by line, chasing receipts and spreadsheets, but moving within a design that accommodates movement. The percentages remain constant; the content flexes. You don't need to know every detail in advance. You only need to know which direction you're heading and which lever to pull when conditions change.

This matters profoundly when life intervenes. Imagine someone loses their job. In a traditional budget, this moment is catastrophic—a total system collapse. The categories crumble, the plan freezes, and the anxiety spikes. But under a bucketed system, there is a pre-existing architecture for adaptation. The Safety bucket provides a buffer, while the Freedom and Joy buckets can be temporarily scaled back. The Essentials bucket receives triage priority. The goal is not to preserve all parts equally, but to *make informed trade-offs from a position of clarity*. Rather than restarting, you recalibrate. Rather than panic, you pivot.

Clarity itself becomes a strategic advantage. One of the most corrosive forces in modern money life is ambiguity. Not knowing how much is safe to spend, not knowing if a holiday jeopardises a mortgage payment, not knowing whether today's indulgence is tomorrow's regret. Ambiguity breeds hesitation, and hesitation corrodes momentum. The bucket framework eliminates ambiguity by making each pound legible. A dinner out from the Joy bucket is not reckless—it's permitted. A sudden car repair that drains the Safety bucket does not derail the whole system—it activates it. *When money has a clear home, your decisions gain moral clarity.*

The model's greatest strength is not in its ability to plan, but in its capacity to *recover*. This may seem counterintuitive in a culture that fetishises goals and productivity, but it's the truth behind enduring financial resilience. People who bounce back fastest from setbacks are not those with the best goals. They are those with the most robust feedback loops. They don't throw away their maps after each detour—they reorient. The five-bucket method is designed precisely for this. It transforms budgeting from a brittle forecast into a responsive, dynamic ecosystem.

There is also a deeper philosophical challenge embedded in traditional goal-setting: the problem of false certainty. Financial plans often require us to guess—about inflation, job prospects, family needs, and more. These projections are not just difficult; they are illusions of control. In contrast, a bucket system acknowledges uncertainty and builds a logic that thrives within it. You don't need to predict the future to be ready for it. *You only need to prepare your structures to flex when it arrives*. In this way, the buckets create a rare fusion of humility and control—humility in accepting unpredictability, and control in knowing how to respond when it strikes.

Contrast this with the prevailing approach taught in much personal finance literature: the linear progress model. This model implies that if you follow the plan, success will follow in sequence. But lives are not linear. A person might pay down debt for months, only to be set back by a single medical bill. A couple may save steadily, then face an unexpected fertility treatment. These aren't failures of planning. They're evidence of life's texture. The bucket model does not punish these deviations. It anticipates them.

Moreover, by reducing the cognitive load of financial management, the bucket system liberates energy for higher-order thinking. When you no longer need to decide from scratch how much to save, spend, or delay each time a transaction arises, you free your mind to focus on strategic questions: Am I building towards what matters? Do my choices reflect my values? Am I living within a structure that supports not just survival, but significance?

That shift—from goal obsession to value alignment—is subtle, but revolutionary. It redefines progress not as reaching some distant benchmark, but as *living today in a way that mirrors your priorities*. This is how wealth becomes visible, not just numerically but psychologically. You feel it not when your net worth hits a round number, but when your actions cease to contradict your ideals. When generosity no longer feels reckless. When rest doesn't trigger guilt. When your money and your mind are moving in the same direction.

For this model to function, of course, there must be discipline. No system erases trade-offs. What the five buckets offer is not permission to spend freely, but *a clear-eyed structure for choosing wisely*. Each bucket is a container of constraints—and it is within these constraints that freedom emerges. The Joy bucket allows indulgence because the Essentials and Future buckets are protected. The Freedom bucket grows only when the Safety bucket is secure. This interdependence creates accountability without micromanagement. It is not about rigid control, but about principled fluidity.

Perhaps the most compelling proof of the bucket model's efficacy is its long-term survivability. Systems that rely on perpetual motivation tend to collapse. Systems that embed automation, reflection, and forgiveness are the ones people actually sustain. The five-bucket model excels here: it is simple enough to grasp, flexible enough to survive volatility, and structured enough to build enduring habits. It requires attention, yes—but not obsession. And in return, it offers a powerful upgrade: from vague goals that crumble under pressure to *a navigational framework that learns, adapts, and endures*.

This is not merely a new budgeting tactic. It is a reframing of how we interact with our money—*not as a series of isolated transactions, but as a mapped landscape of meaning*. With the right map, you don't fear the unknown. You prepare for it. You move through it. And when you fall behind or veer off course—as all of us do—you do not give up. You reroute.

How to Rethink Progress

Progress, when viewed through the lens of most financial culture, is still trapped in a profoundly linear metaphor. Earn more, spend less, invest early, and your graph will move dutifully upwards. A consistent ascent. A climb. A spreadsheet that behaves. But lived experience refuses to comply with this neat trajectory. People don't grow in straight lines. Neither do their incomes, their expenses, their ambitions, or their circumstances. And yet, too many financial systems—and the mental frameworks that surround them—measure progress as if it were a staircase rather than a terrain.

This dissonance is not simply conceptual; it has emotional consequences. When your financial life deviates from the supposed arc of upward motion, even temporarily, the instinctive interpretation is failure. A job lost, a savings account raided for medical bills, a month when spending outpaces earnings—these are treated as reversals, even regressions. The result is a distorted internal narrative that says: "I'm behind." But behind what? Whose timeline? Whose metric? *A fragile definition of progress always produces a brittle sense of self.*

To rethink progress, we must begin by severing its overdependence on numerical accumulation. A rising bank balance, a growing portfolio, or a reduced debt load—these are outcomes. But they are not, in themselves, definitions of progress. True progress is behavioural. It is the alignment between your daily financial actions and your longer-term values. It is not how much you've saved this quarter, but *whether your money is flowing in directions that make your life feel more congruent, more coherent, and more calm.*

Take the example of someone who switches from reactive spending to planned discretionary purchases. Perhaps they still carry the same amount of credit card debt. But their shift from unconscious to intentional spending is *a profound behavioural gain*. Or consider someone who begins allocating even 5% of their income to a Safety bucket after years of living paycheque to paycheque. The account balance may still look modest, but what has shifted is the presence of agency—and that is a deeper form of wealth than the number it produces.

Traditional budgeting models often ignore these forms of invisible growth. They track dollars but not decisions. They celebrate output but not process. The five-bucket system takes a different view. It honours small pivots. It recognises *adaptive fidelity*—the ability to stay true to purpose even when inputs fluctuate. A month when your income drops, but you still maintain your Safety and Essentials allocations? That is not stagnation. That is strategic integrity under pressure. That is progress.

This behavioural definition of growth also allows for *emotional maturity*. Many people oscillate between hyper-control and total avoidance when it comes to money. Either they are rigidly micromanaging every transaction in a spreadsheet, or they are ignoring their finances until something breaks. The five-bucket model invites a middle path: consistent structure without perfectionism. Progress becomes not about controlling every penny, but about *upgrading your defaults*. Are you defaulting now to behaviours that serve your future? Are your instincts becoming more constructive? That shift is progress, even if your net worth hasn't moved.

One of the reasons this reframing is so important is that it protects motivation. When progress is defined exclusively in terms of numerical outcomes, setbacks feel like resets. You wipe the board and start again. This is demoralising and inefficient. But if progress is measured by alignment—by how regularly your money choices reflect your priorities—then setbacks are not erasures. They are part of the system. *You don't start again. You pick up from where you are, equipped with more information.*

This also introduces a powerful insight: *stability is not the same as stagnation*. Many financial plans assume that upward motion is the only direction worth pursuing. But there are seasons of life when holding steady—through illness, caregiving, unemployment, or grief—is a feat of immense resilience. A family who maintains their buckets during a crisis is not failing to progress. They are displaying the very habits that will allow them to build again later. *Plateaus, in this model, are often acts of profound strength.*

Rethinking progress also means allowing for non-monetary indicators of success. Has a couple reduced the frequency of their financial arguments? Has a single parent begun involving their children in bucket-based decision-making? Has a freelance artist moved from panic-driven invoicing to pre-allocating 20% of each payment to a Freedom bucket? These are not small wins. These are structural shifts in how money is related to—and they are the kinds of progress that traditional tools miss entirely.

Critically, the five-bucket system encourages *periodic reflection,* not just continuous tracking. One of its philosophical strengths is that it creates built-in moments for recalibration. You don't wait until something breaks to review your financial life. You schedule it. This cadence of reflection—monthly, quarterly, annually—replaces reactive guilt with proactive learning. And because each bucket has a distinct purpose, you're not just reviewing numbers. You're asking high-quality questions: Are our Essentials creeping up unsustainably? Are we underfunding Joy and risking burnout? Has our Safety bucket become a source of anxiety rather than reassurance?

This becomes a kind of quiet wisdom practice. Not a performance. Not a race. But a rhythm. A way of staying in active relationship with your resources, without becoming consumed by them. *Progress, then, becomes not a destination to reach, but a habit of returning.*

Of course, this model challenges many of the cultural norms embedded in finance. We are still bombarded by headlines that celebrate extremes—early retirees, six-figure savers, debt-free declarations. These stories often obscure the messier, slower, more ordinary trajectories of real people building thoughtful financial lives. The five-bucket framework does not oppose ambition, but it insists on grounding it in sustainability. *The question is not how fast you can build wealth, but how well your daily systems support your values without sacrificing your well-being.*

The payoff for this redefinition of progress is multidimensional. It creates a more accurate picture of where you are. It maintains motivation even during financially flat seasons. And it gives you tools to *celebrate movement that matters,* not just metrics that impress. It also protects against one of the quietest financial traps: success that doesn't feel successful. Many high earners find themselves bewildered by their own dissatisfaction. Their bank accounts grow, but their sense of control, meaning, or joy does not. Why? Because the growth was not aligned. Their financial life expanded, but their inner life didn't.

Behavioural alignment changes this. When your income supports a life you recognise as intentional, your sense of satisfaction is not tethered to external validation. You know, in quiet, private ways, that your system is working—even if no one else sees it. This is a quieter, less cinematic form of progress. But it is also deeper, more enduring, and ultimately more honest.

To measure growth through behaviour rather than balance sheets is not to lower the bar. It is to *raise the standard for what counts as meaningful success*. It requires attentiveness. It rewards self-awareness. And it produces a financial life that is not only functional, but *fulfilling*. If you know where your money is going, and that it is going in ways that reflect who you are and what you care about, then you are not "behind." You are not "off track." You are progressing—because you are participating.

And that is the metric that matters most.

Periodic Rebalancing: A Ritual, Not a Reaction

Most people only engage with their financial systems under pressure—when something breaks, when anxiety spikes, or when an external event forces attention inward. The problem is not that people don't care about their finances; it's that they've been conditioned to relate to them reactively rather than rhythmically. Financial reflection becomes an emergency activity, not a regular practice. This habit of crisis-driven management produces chronic instability, where money feels like a moving target rather than a responsive tool. *What the five-bucket model offers, at its core, is not only a structure for allocation—but a cadence for reflection.* And that rhythm matters more than most people realise.

To understand why, we must first reframe what rebalancing is. In investing, portfolio rebalancing is the act of periodically adjusting allocations to maintain intended ratios—protecting against drift caused by market fluctuations. It's a neutral, mechanical process. No judgment, no panic, just course correction. Personal finances deserve the same neutrality, yet most people approach budget rebalancing with guilt, dread, or frustration. The implication is always that something has gone wrong. But real life is dynamic. Categories shift. Priorities evolve. Expenses emerge. *Rebalancing is not a signal of failure. It's a discipline of responsiveness.* It allows you to stay tethered to your intentions even as your reality flexes.

The genius of the five-bucket system lies in its modularity. Each bucket—Essentials, Safety, Joy, Freedom, and Growth—represents not just a category of spending but a category of meaning. When you rebalance, you're not merely adjusting figures; you're recalibrating your values. Has your Essentials bucket expanded because of inflation, or lifestyle creep? Is your Joy bucket being starved while your Safety bucket overflows out of fear? Has your Freedom bucket (often used for paying down debt or buying time) become a neglected afterthought because your income has grown, and you've stopped prioritising autonomy? These are not technical questions. They are philosophical ones. And yet, they can be answered numerically—if the system invites regular, reflective engagement.

Rebalancing, in this context, becomes a kind of financial hygiene. Like brushing your teeth or getting an annual health check, it's not about drama or excitement. It's about maintenance—small, repeated acts that prevent decay. The goal is not to achieve a perfect configuration, but to remain in dialogue with your own needs. Because those needs are not static. A new job might increase your Essentials but decrease your Freedom. A growing family might require more from your Safety and less from your Joy. A period of burnout may demand an intentional redirection of funds toward restorative travel, therapy, or time off—paid for with funds previously earmarked for Growth.

This regular dialogue with your buckets protects against emotional distortion. In the absence of structured rebalancing, people tend to operate from financial mood swings—oscillating between scarcity and overconfidence, rigidity and indulgence. But when recalibration is scheduled—monthly, quarterly, or annually—it introduces proportionality. You're less likely to overreact to a single overspend, or catastrophise a temporary dip in income. You are not guessing; you are checking in. *And when you check in consistently, the story you tell yourself about your money becomes more accurate, more grounded, and more generous.*

What does this look like in practice? For many, the most powerful rebalancing ritual happens on the last Sunday of each month. They sit down—alone or with a partner—and review their allocations against what actually occurred. They ask: Did I fund what I said I would? Did any unexpected expenses arise that require a forward shift in priorities? Do my buckets still reflect my current reality and future hopes? Are there any buckets that are consistently being ignored, or ones that have become bloated without intention? This ritual often takes no more than 30 minutes. But it offers something rare: *a sustained, non-reactive relationship with money*.

The contrast to this rhythm is everywhere. Reactive financial behaviour is the norm. We notice our finances only when there's a problem—an overdraft fee, a declined card, a savings goal missed. In this model, budgeting becomes punishment. The spreadsheet appears only after the damage is done, like a forensic tool for self-blame. But when you turn budgeting into a ritual—calm, repeated, structured—you shift from regret to inquiry. And inquiry is far more productive than judgment.

This shift also matters at a neurological level. When financial decisions are made under duress, the brain's prefrontal cortex—the seat of reasoning and executive function—often goes offline. We default to either fight, flight, or freeze. That's why some people panic-spend, others shut down completely, and some lash out. But a ritualised rebalancing schedule creates psychological safety. You're not ambushed by your finances. You're meeting them on your terms, in a context of calm. This psychological shift compounds over time. You begin to associate financial review with agency, not fear. With learning, not loss. *And that emotional tone shapes every future decision.*

There is also an important social dimension to rebalancing. For couples, families, or business partners who share finances, periodic recalibration fosters transparency. It becomes the designated space for renegotiating shared priorities, resolving tensions, and resetting expectations. Without these moments, resentment builds. One partner silently cuts back on personal spending while the other continues discretionary purchases. One parent prioritises savings for children's education while the other focuses on home upgrades. The buckets become battlegrounds. But when recalibration is normalised—say, at the start of each quarter—these tensions are addressed before they calcify.

The system, in this way, becomes not just financial infrastructure, but *relational scaffolding*.

What's more, rebalancing demystifies the idea of financial change. Many people resist adjusting their systems because they feel that doing so invalidates past decisions. But adaptability is not an admission of failure. It's a mark of maturity. The fact that your current allocations are no longer serving you is not a problem—it's a signal. One that becomes visible only if you're regularly looking. In this way, the five-bucket framework behaves like a compass, not a cage. It points you back to alignment. And every time you rebalance, you are practising that alignment—reinforcing it, fine-tuning it, and evolving it.

The resistance to rebalancing often comes from perfectionism. People believe they should "get it right" the first time. But no financial system is static, because no life is static. Your buckets are not commandments; they are agreements. Agreements that must be revisited as conditions change. When you accept this, you replace the shame of "I failed my budget" with the clarity of "My budget no longer fits, and that's useful information."

Ultimately, what the five-bucket model offers is a scaffolding for financial rhythm. Not rules, but rituals. Not rigidity, but responsiveness. A healthy financial life is not one that never wobbles—it's one that has systems in place to notice the wobble early, and correct gently. And that correction, done regularly and without drama, becomes one of the most powerful habits a person can build.

You're not rebalancing to fix something broken. You're rebalancing to keep something alive. That's the distinction that matters. Because a living system—a thoughtful, adaptive, recalibrated system—can weather storms. It can grow with you. It can absorb setbacks and still remain functional. *And when your financial system is alive, you don't just survive. You sustain.*

The Wealth You Can Feel

The most valuable form of wealth is often the least measured. It doesn't appear on bank statements or tax returns. It cannot be quantified in spreadsheets or explained in asset allocation charts. Yet it shapes everything. This is the wealth of clarity—the quiet confidence of knowing where your money is, what it's doing, and why. It is the wealth of emotional safety—the felt sense that you are not at the mercy of your income, but in right relationship with it. It is the wealth of time, choice, and dignity—the freedom to live without financial confusion polluting every decision. In a world obsessed with numeric accumulation, *this kind of wealth remains profoundly underrated*. But it is this form that endures, stabilises, and liberates.

Too often, the language of personal finance collapses into a singular metric: net worth. That figure, while informative, tells only a fraction of the story. It cannot capture whether you sleep well at night, whether you feel safe spending money on what matters to you, whether your finances align with your values or fracture them. Two people with identical net worths may live radically different financial lives—one in a fog of anxiety, shame, and chaos; the other with composure, purpose, and flow. The difference is not found in the number. It's found in the system beneath the number. *Structure creates experience.* And the five-bucket method is built to restore financial clarity not just as an idea, but as a felt reality.

At its heart, the five-bucket framework is not just a budgeting tool. It is a philosophy of financial self-ownership. By giving every pound a place—across Essentials, Safety, Joy, Freedom, and Growth—it transforms the act of managing money from a reactive chore into a proactive ritual. This ritual doesn't just improve outcomes. It alters your sense of agency. Instead of wondering whether you can afford something, you know where to look. Instead of guessing at trade-offs, you see them clearly. *Ambiguity becomes allocation. Hesitation becomes intentionality.* That transformation is not merely cognitive. It is emotional.

Consider the psychological impact of the Joy bucket alone. In conventional budgets, discretionary spending is either discouraged or left vague—resulting in guilt-laced decisions and a recurring sense of indulgence versus discipline. But when joy has a designated place in your system, it becomes legitimate. Whether it's a massage, a birthday dinner, or a new book, the act is no longer weighed against your moral worthiness—it's funded, planned, respected. The emotional experience of spending shifts from recklessness or self-justification to celebration. The wealth you feel isn't just the ability to buy—it's the ability to do so without mental friction.

Similarly, the Safety bucket redefines preparedness. Emergency funds are often spoken about in abstract terms—three to six months of expenses, held in a passive account, rarely revisited until disaster strikes. But when Safety is built into your active system, not siloed from it, *you stop fearing emergencies as events that break your finances*. You begin to treat them as foreseeable seasons that your system can adapt to. This adaptive confidence—rooted in allocation, not income—is a psychological stabiliser. People with vastly different earnings can both experience the same sense of readiness, if their buckets are set and honoured. In this way, the model neutralises income-based shame and replaces it with system-based strength.

This strength is also visible in the way the five-bucket system aligns behaviour with belief. Too many people report a chronic dissonance between what they value and how they spend. They want to prioritise family, but their calendar is crowded with work to meet rising expenses. They want to be generous, but fear running out of money. They want to pursue a passion project, but feel tethered to debt. These are not failures of willpower. They are symptoms of misalignment. And misalignment breeds distress. *When your money moves in ways that contradict your values, your nervous system notices*. It produces chronic background noise—doubt, resentment, fatigue.

By contrast, when your system reflects your priorities, something quiet but profound occurs: *you begin to trust yourself again.* That trust compounds. Each spending decision reinforces your internal narrative: "I am someone who funds what matters." The shift is not instantaneous, but it is cumulative. Every transfer into the Growth bucket affirms a future vision. Every spend from the Freedom bucket confirms your right to design your own life. Every allocation into Joy protects your humanity in a world that often treats financial prudence as a synonym for deprivation. *That is not just budgeting. That is self-respect in motion.*

There's also the relational impact of this model. Money is one of the most common sources of tension in families and partnerships. Not because people don't agree on values—but because they lack a shared language for expressing them financially. The five-bucket structure becomes that language. When two people say, "We need to increase our Safety bucket," they are not arguing; they are aligning. When one partner says, "I'd like to redirect some of our Joy funds to Freedom this quarter," they are not issuing a demand; they are offering a proposal. The emotional tone of financial communication softens when it is framed structurally. Clarity becomes collaboration. *And collaboration is a form of wealth in itself.*

What is perhaps most transformative about the bucket system is that it displaces perfection as the metric of success. Instead of asking, "Did I get everything right?" the more productive question becomes, "Am I moving in a direction that honours what matters?" That is a question rooted in values, not vanity. And it is answered not once, but rhythmically—through reflection, review, and recalibration. In this way, the five-bucket model becomes a container for personal growth as much as financial stewardship. You are not chasing an arbitrary goalpost. You are deepening your fluency in your own financial language. You are tracking progress not by what you accumulate, but by *how often your behaviour aligns with your belief system*.

This has implications beyond the financial realm. When people describe feeling "rich," they are often pointing to something less tangible than money itself. They speak of calm. Of agency. Of space to think, decide, create. They speak of the absence of dread when opening a bank app. Of the ease of funding a spontaneous dinner without anxiety. Of the dignity of being able to help someone else without destabilising their own system. These moments are small, but they are cumulative. They represent not just financial capability, but emotional sovereignty.

That is the kind of wealth this model seeks to build. Not just accounts that grow, but lives that feel whole. Not just plans that work on paper, but systems that hold under pressure. Not just financial wins, but *financial wellness*—the enduring ability to act with clarity, freedom, and intention, even in the face of challenge. That wellness is not a byproduct of wealth. It is a dimension of it. And it is available sooner than most people think—not at some hypothetical future income level, but at the moment your money starts flowing through a system that reflects your truth.

Ultimately, what you feel in your financial life matters as much as what you earn. *Because how you feel determines how you behave. And how you behave determines what you build*. The wealth you can feel is not a consolation prize. It is the prize. A system that offers clarity, protects your values, and adapts as you do is not a luxury. It is the core infrastructure for a life lived with composure and coherence. And that, more than any number, is the definition of being financially well.

About the Author

Daniel Hayes writes for people who want their lives to make sense—not just in their heads, but in their calendars, wallets, and choices. With a calm voice and a clear mind, he explores the intersection of systems thinking, everyday psychology, and practical living. His work focuses on helping readers build resilient, intentional structures—whether in how they spend their time, manage their money, or pursue meaning. Hayes brings a quietly radical message: you don't need more hustle, just a better map. When he's not writing, he's often sketching out frameworks, hiking in quiet places, or helping others untangle complexity in search of clarity.

www.ingramcontent.com/pod-product-compliance
Lightning Source LLC
Chambersburg PA
CBHW031338230926
51848CB00002B/284
* 9 7 8 9 3 7 1 7 7 1 8 9 4 *